LEAVING MY MARK

Wind in the Reeds Publishing
www.windinthereedspublishing.com

Copyright © 2020 by Eloria Elliot

First Edition – July 26, 2020
ALL RIGHTS RESERVED

Font: FF Parango
Illustrations: Adobe Photoshop Watercolor Brushes by McBadshoes

ISBN 9-781734-917604

LEAVING MY MARK

A Journey of Loss and Letting Go

Eloria Elliot

PATHWAYS

Sometimes
our journeys paint
pathways
through dark places,
forcing us
to walk the hurting highways
of heartache.

But, in brokenness
we all are bound together
because we own
hearts
that crack and chip
when life throws
trial and tragedy at us.

And the interweaving
of words into
stories and poetry and songs
helps us to
heal and cope with
our losses, our yearnings,
and our bereavements.

Through the sharing of these sorrows,
we gain understanding,
give empathy, and
go forth into the world
realizing at last
that we are
not alone.

Preface

A journey may begin with map in hand and a detailed itinerary, or it may take you in hand without your approval and force you to tread down a path you did not plan or desire. However it goes, a journey may often bring exposure to many unknowns along the way as you travel toward a place (whether spiritual, emotional or physical) you have yet to be.

This is a true story told in poetic fashion because that is how I processed the pain, sorrow and tragedy and their after-effects. All that happened is real. So here follows a memoir of sorts, sharing my steps and stumbles, heights and depths, tears and joys – all lending their kaleidoscopic colors to the landscapes of this long and labyrinthine journey.

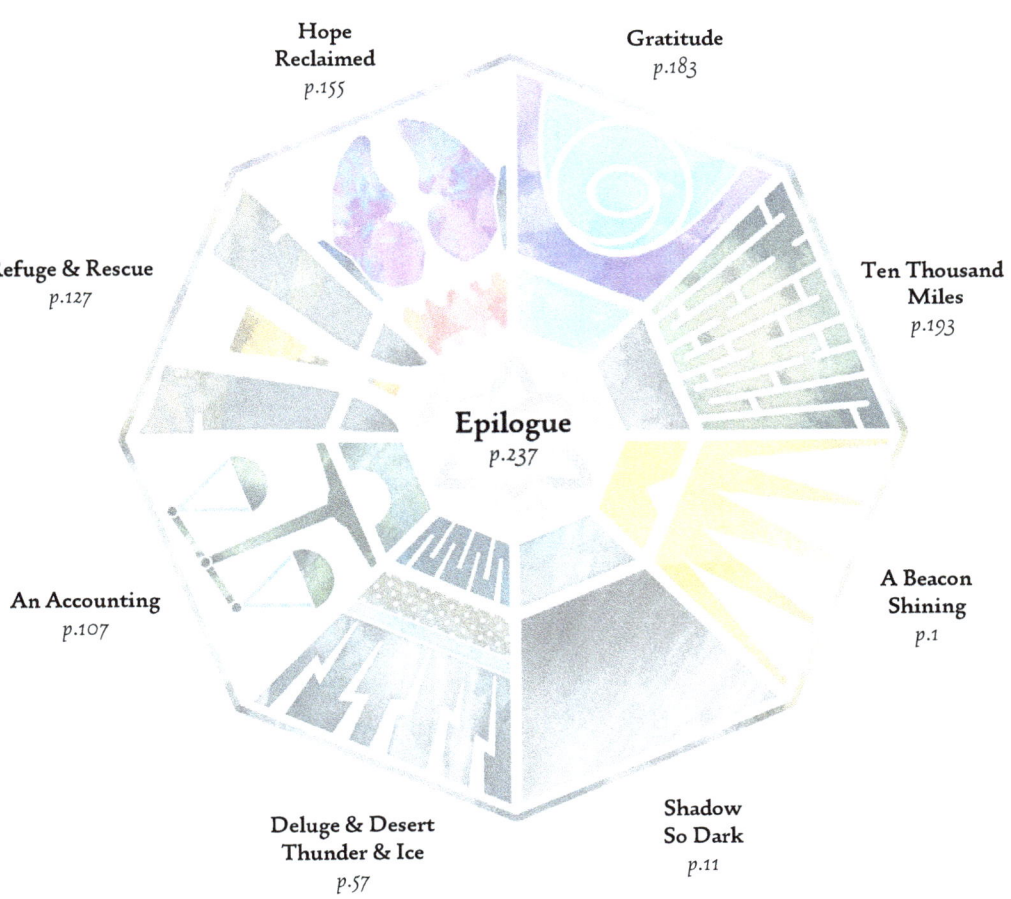

Table of Contents

- Hope Reclaimed — p.155
- Gratitude — p.183
- Ten Thousand Miles — p.193
- A Beacon Shining — p.1
- Shadow So Dark — p.11
- Deluge & Desert Thunder & Ice — p.57
- An Accounting — p.107
- Refuge & Rescue — p.127
- Epilogue — p.237

Prologue

DYING DAY

I didn't know
his pledge to me
would end that day.

But not because
of a promise broken.

No,
not that.

He kept his word
as I did mine,
and we knit
these words together –

For all time,
we thought,
as the dawn christened us
with its rosy light.

Then one day our world
tipped over
without warning;
one of us
would never get back up.

"I will love you till
my dying day,"
he had told me
so many years ago.

And he did.

A BEACON SHINING

MARK

One day
I met Mark,
and it was like opening the door
to a world
where delightful discoveries
bloomed across
a landscape of
mesmerizing mystery.

At first,
I was afraid of him.
He was tall, handsome, athletic, self-confident and
smart.

So, I avoided him.

But, it didn't work.

I soon found out that
he was
not to be feared, but respected;
not to be ignored, but adored;
not to be taken lightly, but seriously.

We fell in love.

And the adventure of
getting to know each other
renovated our
lives.

I was an introverted country girl;
he was an ambitious
city boy.

I had lived in one place
most of my life.

He had lived all over
the world.

I taught him how to appreciate
sunsets and trees and nature.

He tried to teach me how to . . .
tolerate cities.

He was a patient guy.
Impatience was my middle name,
or first name, depending.

He knew something about
everything.
I imagined everything out of
nothing.

He liked anything to do with
science and math.
I ran screaming from
such subjects.

Numbers and their problems
brought a gleam
to his eyes.

Words and the stories
they could create
made my eyes
sparkle . . . I think.
(I can only surmise that it was so.)

Together,
we could conquer
the world.

And on our wedding day,
the conquest
commenced.

A Beacon Shining

Mark knew Jesus Christ
as his Savior
and his faith in his Lord
untangled
the confusion of my life,
swiping away the snares
of uncertainty
and showing me the Way
to find true Grace
and Mercy.

Our marriage and our children
emblazoned our lives
with joy; a blessing that
strengthened us
when hardship threatened
our peace.

Because of Mark
I finally realized
my lifelong dream to
travel the world.

Because of him
I found out what true love
meant and I learned
the definition
through weighted words
framed by action.

The trust I understood only in
small letters,
grew until it became
Trust with a
capital T.

Mark taught me the deeper
meaning behind
sacrificial giving and
service to others.

We were not perfect;
not as a couple nor as
individuals.

Our ups and downs
kept us on our toes, or
posteriors –
whatever happened
to be the case.

We weathered many storms
together; whether
thunder or turmoil,
we never lacked for
excitement.

Our final adventure
came . . . unexpectedly.

Mark's sense of humor
was the last thing
we shared
before tragedy
interfered.

Neither of us knew
that it was to be
our last moment
together.

Mark was my hero,
and I never failed to give him
lots of opportunities to
come to my rescue.

His armor beamed so brightly
because he poured
his love out so
lavishly.

Still his armor is shining.

It is a beacon
for our journey that
emboldens us to
live out
extravagant love
so that one day
we might leave legacies
as luminous
as his.

FLAWS, FOIBLES AND FORBEARANCE

So human
were we as we struggled and strived,
fought and connived,
helped and healed and hugged.

Never perfect
were we as we blamed and boasted,
argued and roasted,
laughed and loved and lived.

Always trying
were we as we forgot and forgave,
grumbled and behaved,
prayed and planned and played.

Just us
were we as we flourished and failed,
succeeded and prevailed,
confided and cared and consoled.

THE TWENTIETH YEAR

Newlyweds no longer,
but
something better –
togetherness
impacted
by longstanding
commitment involving:
the trivial, the annoying
and the goofy,
kaleidoscopic conversations,
animated arguments,
romance and finance,
the humdrums
of
life,
unexpected adventures
as well as
boring routines,
encouragement and shoulder pats,
stubbornness and compromise,
three children,
brow mopping,
nerve wracking,
gift presenting,
along-side working,
game playing,
bills,
praying, dancing, silly song singing –
all the accumulations
of
marriage
celebrated on the
twentieth anniversary
in Hawaii,
one year before
our last year
together.

SHADOW SO DARK

DILEMMA

At first
it was a mere
interference
disguised
as a commoner.

The usual route
was pursued
to address such an
annoyance.

And that was it,
we thought.
But, it did not
go away.

Instead,
it not only interrupted,
It monopolized.

So, in the wee hours
of the morning,
we succumbed to
an ER visit in
the hopes of
resolution.

Hours later
with prescription in hand,
we returned home
thinking all was
well.

But no,
Mark's condition
worsened throughout
that day and night, and
in the predawn hours
we wondered
what to do.

Should we wait
for a doctor's appointment
or go back to
the ER?

After some debate,
prodded by an impending
urgency, we
chose a path.

We revisited
the ER and submitted
to a doctor's
counsel, trusting
in the treatment
he prescribed.

I was sent
to the waiting room
with the assurance that
the procedure
would be successful
and succinct.

But time plodded by –
there was nothing
succinct about it.

 *Shadow So Dark*

Pandemonium
prevailed,
as did Death
soon thereafter.

In the aftermath
I pondered the possibility
of a different
outcome
had we only taken
another path.

And thus began
the torture
of pitting one choice
against another,
a dilemma
no longer valid, yet
armed with
condemnation.

BETRAYAL

A chance meeting
because of pain, of fear
and two lives
are twined
together
by a slender, silken strand
from the web
of what could
destroy them both.

A doctor. A patient.
One giving hope to,
the other putting trust in.
And then havoc
is wreaked.

In an instant
a time-passenger
is halted,
and the balance is tipped.
Despair presents itself
while trust quickly departs.

Truth is hastily
hemmed in,
allowing confusion and chaos
to reign freely.
Alas, the patient's quest
for life is lost in
disarray.

Disbelief disarms
the mind.
Shock stuns
the heart.

And Betrayal
comes out from
the shadows.

HELPLESS

Watching you suffer,
not understanding why,
not knowing how to help you,
feeling useless in your agony.

Your nightmare
becomes my horror;
our shared terrors meet
and embrace each other.

Fear entangles itself
with reason until
confused panic overshadows
all thinking and feeling.

The clutching fingers
of doubt begin to tighten
their grip on our hope
of a brimming future together.

My mind reels
in a conundrum of spiraling
scenarios depicting how I can
rescue us both from this madness.

Oh, how powerless
we are together in this storm
that ravages you and revolts me
as I witness your decline.

I cannot
ease your pain nor stop
the thieving disease that steals
away the essence of your life.

Shadow So Dark

I cannot
shelter you from the harm
nor shield you from the mistakes
that have taken your breath away.

I cannot
bring you back from the brink
nor can I invoke
you from the void.

For I am
helpless, helpless, helpless –
so infuriatingly unable to reclaim you
from these cruel calamities.

CORRIDORS

In the hallways of the hospital
untold stories
play out
all around me as I walk
this maze of corridors.

I survey a scene before me –
a family clusters together and
cries out
in their shock and in their grief
as they grapple with the unimaginable.

Turning the corner, I come across
a nurse in cheerful uniform who purposefully
shuts out
all other distractions but the one
to whom she is tending.

A few faltering steps further I notice
a stone-faced husband trying to
block out
his fears and emotions
as he contemplates the prognosis for his wife.

As I continue my somber stroll I observe
two doctors, heads bent together, attempting to
figure out
what treatment to prescribe
for an unforgiving disease.

I drift about in a daze and bump into
a man I met in the waiting room; he
sings out
with joy, for he just learned that
his sister will recover.

Unintentionally, I find myself walking beside
an agitated couple whose patience
runs out
because their little one
suffers such underserved pain.

On and on I roam – a ghostly vagabond
searching for answers and hope; I soon
tire out
from the narratives I witness, unwritten
and scattered within these watchful walls.

As I meander along,
losing and finding my way over and over, I
look out
for the hurting and the healed,
sensing a kinship between us.

Like invisible tendrils, our desperations,
our longings and our fears
reach out
and entwine us all together
in these chronicles of the corridors.

CLASSICAL

Numb
because of the sorrow,
shocked,
because of the pain,
I turn off my heart and mind.

Night
cloaks the ritual of my departures.
Forgetting
where I had parked the car,
I listen for my car's answering chirp.

Reunited
with this refuge on wheels,
reclining
in its manufactured comfort,
I breathe in the artificial calmness.

Silence
envelopes me for the moment,
serenity
prods me to forget the chaos
of the Intensive Care.

Exhausted
by an overwhelming hopelessness,
refusing
to believe the unbelievable,
I fight the urge to self-destruct.

Turning
on the radio, desirous of distraction,
searching
for an alternate reality,
I insulate myself from the nightmare.

Voices
sing out over the airwaves,
telling
tales I no longer can process,
their words inadequate to reach my brain.

Desperately
I scan the stations at my fingertips,
finding,
at last, an instrumental escape
to sooth my fraying soul.

Relaxing,
I listen to this balm of euphony.
Revived,
my heart absorbs the musical elixir;
and I am consoled by the classical.

THE FINAL ANSWER

In the anguish of the hour,
the hour
when the answer comes,
I shrink back
afraid
not wanting to know,
not wanting my world
to fall apart
and scatter
like the pieces of a puzzle
tossed aside.

But finally,
what cannot be denied,
what cannot be ignored,
stands in front of me
and stares me down.
I cannot turn away
now that
my harrowed heart has been
ambushed
by the news, the results –
the final answer.

The truth,
like wormwood,
is forced upon me
and I must swallow it.
So I do,
at which time the real
suffering
begins: the lamenting,
the weeping, the inescapable
torture
that assaults the soul.

In the loss, the parting,
in the mute goodbye,
Grief
crowns itself and reigns
over this capsized
kingdom
built from the pieces
of a heart imploded.

No matter,
for I am lost now
and care not whether
my disbanded
heart is assembled
ever again.

Broken
because I will have to bury
the one who held
my puzzled fragments
together.

Oh, the anguish of this hour
when the final answer
descends upon me
like the ashes
from a burning
palace.

How I will always
remember
this truth that strangles me,
tormenting my mind,
turning my heart,
taking away
my words, my reasons
and
extinguishing
my hope.

THE LACK OF YOU

When you are gone,
who will I be
without
my favorite half
of our whole?

What is this world
when your footsteps
no longer
echo in hallways
or leave prints in the sand?

Who shall I run to
when you are not to be found?
Loneliness
will enfold me instead
of your loving arms.

Where will my compass be
when you are not here,
absent
from my sight and side
as I struggle through life?

Why should I keep going
after you have gone away?
Emptiness
now claims my heart
because of the lack of you.

TELL THEM

Watching them sit around
the patio table
doing their homework, chatting
companionably, my heart aches.

I have news to tell my children
that will shake them
and cause tears to spill from
their beautiful, trusting eyes.

There is such a peace around them
as they enjoy the lovely day,
believing that their dad
is going to be okay.

But, that is not to be the case
as the doctors informed me today;
and now I must explain to
my children this tragic truth.

They do not yet know
that their adoring dad will never
again joke around with them, or play
games and sports and sing silly songs.

They do not yet know
that their dad's bear-hugging,
protecting, encouraging, teaching,
and praying ways will be no more.

My pounding heart echoes through me
as I take a deep breath and approach
my children, hating that I must tell them
what they do not want to know.

BRING HIM BACK

Betrayal
loosens its grip
once the deed is done
and the harm has come.

Tossed
on the hardened ground
are the broken wings
of a life and its dreams.

Apologies
mask the hidden mistakes
that took away the breath
until nothing else was left.

Sleep
takes a twisted turn
for brain waves exist not
and thoughts therein have stopped.

Returning
to who he once was
can never be again –
there is only one remaining end.

Prayers
are lifted heavenward,
pleading for a miracle;
however, a maelstrom unfurls.

Acceptance
of this uncharted loss
is a course that must be tried
for this reality will not be denied.

Shadow So Dark

Forgiveness
is the one true protection
against a cold and bitter heart,
and keeps a light on in the dark.

Mercy
links the betrayed to betrayer
with a cord to unite
instead of a continual strife.

Regrets
have no power over peace
and cannot undo the past,
nor can they ever bring him back.

THE CIRCLE

Chairs are arranged in a circle
and we sit on them,
arranging ourselves side-by-side
like soldiers awaiting
orders.

We must meet in this way
to face each other –
meeting to discuss a horrific fate
from which there is no
escape.

One by one we give our opinions,
each voice strained,
giving anguished words that cost much
to hear and to
ponder.

As we share we are overcome by the grief
that binds us together,
sharing the common cord
of an unavoidable
truth.

Life was taken from our loved one
long before his time,
taking him from us and plunging
him into a brain-extinguished
existence.

We must decide how much longer
he should remain so;
deciding, we unanimously agree
to let him go
Home.

Our hearts break with the realization
that he is already gone,
breaking apart our lives and
leaving behind an empty
place.

Finally, we pray to our Father,
who surrounds us in our mourning.
Praying, we ask for the strength
to endure life outside our
Circle.

PAPER CRANES

Waiting, waiting
for the worst,
idle hands
(my children's hands)
grasp for paper
to fold, to crease,
to bend to their will
because
their highest prayer
will not secure
their deepest desire.

For dying nearby
is their father
and they can not
save him.
The manifestation
of their anguish
arrays the table tops –
tiny paper cranes,
white and delicate,
like crumbs
from a birthday cake.

Only
no candles
brighten the darkness
and no songs
gladden the heart;
and there is
not enough paper
to make a thousand
little cranes
to grant the one wish
of my children.

LAST BREATH

Resisting it for his sake,
or is it for mine?

Because a world without him
cannot exist
in my heart,
in my mind,
in my soul.

Yet, it is coming . . .
this world.

Each second, each minute
brings it closer to its
genesis.

And I hang on and hang on
to what once was:
to him alive and well,
laughing, joking, loving, giving . . .
being.

But, no more it seems –
for he lies there swallowed
by a dying sleep,
released from the tangled web
of machinery.

What beauty is this that my kiss
cannot revive?

The writing in the Book of Life
draws near the end of its
sentence for him.

I feel its fatal approach;
the last stroke of the pen casts
its final flourish.

I look at him.
I memorize him.
I anguish this encroaching
bereavement.

And then it happens:
a hushing –
      one last pause
           before
the chilling and concrete
conclusion.

His time has come
and I am there
to behold
his last breath.

THE UNCLASPING

I held his hand,
    but
        he did not hold back.

I beheld his face,
    but
        mine he could not see.

I spoke words of love,
    but
        his voice remained silent.

I wept tears of sorrow,
    but
        his tears would not fall.

I whispered out his name,
    but
        his ears remained deaf.

I watched his end draw near.

    I heard his heartbeat stop.

        I felt his hand grow cold.

The stillness.

    The quiet.

I unclasped my hand
        from his . . .
            It took a long time.

THE PLEAD

I watch Death
infiltrate
my husband's body,
taking its toll
by demolishing the artistry
of all that he is.

"Heal him," I plead.
"Nothing is impossible
for you, Father God.
I know you can,
I know it!"

Ceaselessly, my petition echoes
in and out of my mind.

I wait and I wait.

I want to bestow my breath
to my soulmate
so he too can draw
in the air.

If only I could
lend him the beats
from my heart and the waves
from my brain.
I would! I would!
"Oh, please God
take from me and give to him
so we both can live."

But the day surrenders its light
and the darkness of night
looms ominous.

At the awful last,
Death swallows Mark's life
like ravenous quicksand.

I offer up all that I am
and pray, "Raise him from
the dead, Lord.
Raise him!"

My life has been painted
with the colors
of his love,
with his thoughts and dreams,
his laughter, compassion
and strength.
"Let not the colors fade," I cry.

But the canvas
is shaded in grey
and the paintbrush
is laid aside.

"Is this my prayer's answer?
Is this it?!"

I witness only
the quiet
and the cold
and the empty.

And I wait and wonder
what is there left to wait for?

Tomorrow's palette is
scraped bare
as defeat takes hostage
my hope.

WALKING OUT

"Take as long as you need,"
says the sympathetic nurse.

My eyes refuse to
turn away from the
still form
of my husband –
no more to struggle,
no more to fight
death.

But, I force myself
to survey the room
we decorated with cards,
Bible verses,
and family photos
arranged like a
cloud of witnesses
to encourage, to proclaim love,
to persuade him
to come back
to us.

One by one,
I stack the cards
and peel the pictures
off the walls.

And then I rest my gaze
back upon him.

Shadow So Dark

Standing beside his bed,
I embrace him
with my soul;
in my heart
no one can see
that I am not
letting go.

Finally, I kiss him
and hug him the best I can,
allowing our life together
to replay in my mind.

On an impulse,
I place a tiny paper crane
made by one of our children
into his cold hand,
though one thousand
winged wishes will not
bring him back.

Hesitantly,
I back out of the room –
my view of him ever
vanishing
as I begin the
long walk out of this
place of sorrows.

UNTITLED

Unplugged
are the machines
that brought breath to
him.

Unbroken
is the heart-line
that showed life in
him.

Unwavering
is the silence
that envelops
him.

Unyielding
is the black earth
that will embrace
him.

Undying
are the tributes
that will remember
him.

ALTAR

A place
of beginnings –
a baptism,
a dedication,
a promise to
love.

And a place of
endings – a casket,
a memorial, a
death do us
part.

O Altar,
where once I smiled
with joy in your sunlight,
I now tremble with
grief in your
shadow.

Such purpose
you serve that so many
smiles and tears can
intermingle
to offer greetings
at life's dawn
and bid farewell
at its dusk.

How you mark
our days,

Altar!

UNTIL

Looking down into the cavity
where he rests
encased in an impenetrable cell,
I see what I could not see before:
the torment hiding behind the vow,
"until death do you part".

The solidity of this revelation
casts it somber shadow
upon me as I surrender
a solitary rose of remembrance.
It graces the stoic casket
with a pronouncement of finality.

My husband is
not truly in the grave,
for I know that he is now living
in the presence of his Savior.
But, here I am without him, feeling
as if I have lost the only home I ever had.

My soul feels threadbare,
like a tattered patchwork quilt
useless in its task
to bring comfort and warmth.
The wound in the earth mirrors
the hollow in my heart.

The graveside service concludes gently
with the pastor's prayer.
Family and friends hesitantly drift away,
their words of condolence fading in
the distance. It is then that I am introduced
to the life that comes after "until".

EVERY SHOVELFUL OF DIRT

The gapingness of his grave
is wide and deep, oh so courageously deep.

It is time now to put an end
to the vacancy that occupies this chasm.

His final bed shimmers like
black diamonds hidden in a cave.

But instead of mining for stones of great value
we must camouflage this lost treasure.

So, we take this deposit of untold worth
and invest it into the dark domain of the earth.

Stepping back, we wait and watch as the
misplaced soil is returned to its rightful residence.

One shovelful follows another, delivering
these scattered dust worlds back to their grounded galaxies.

This hurt mountain-hill of unearthed turf
creepingly retreats back into its longed-for abyss.

And the unanswerable void reaches ever upwards
to gain new territory from the empty air.

Gravity calls to each signature of soil
conducting a symphony of deepening darkfall.

I listen to this music of the earth
and I hear the singing of its taunting dirge.

On and on wails the shoveled dirt
of what once was and of what will never be.

Earthly entities dance together
intermingling to form an impenetrable waltz.

And as the dancers gain momentum, they
fortify the barrier between the living and the dead.

How they mock me, these crumbs of the earth,
caring only that they separate me from the one I love.

I can do no more than solely stand,
repulsively rooted to the ground I so resent.

Shovelful upon shovelful, and then at last
the culmination of cover up is accomplished.

Finality, in the dust-filled silence,
has claimed its ultimate reign on this burial ground.

"It is over," declares the carefully placed
mantle of perfectly manicured sod.

I reluctantly step forward and kneel down
upon this hallowed ground of disenchantment.

"Until the end," I had promised.
"I will stay with you until the very end."

And so it is finished, as duly witnessed by
each and every shovelful of dirt.

 Shadow So Dark

BOXED IN

Little alleyways
hemmed in
with boxes
filled with the stuff
of living.

Still unpacked
weeks later because
of the demise
of the owner.

Death stopped
the daily doings –
no routine had yet
been decreed,
so soon after moving
had the upset
occurred.

Not just an upset,
but an end –
never to be revived
again.

Death diminishes
any reason or desire
to unpack
at all.

Why bother.

Life isn't life
anymore.

Boxes tip, trip, and
block the path;
here and there
shutting out
the sunshine,
bringing on the
shadows.

Immersed
in cluttered emptiness,
surrounded by
things clamoring
to get out
of their trappings,
I sit and stare.

I stop caring.

Who I really
want
is buried deep
within the earth,

boxed in

as am I

above ground.

GOSSAMER SHADOW

Ghostly footfalls
tingle the air
searching for someone
who isn't there.

Watching the shine
of sparkling dust,
hoping for answers
that she can trust.

She sighs her pain
and slips into
gossamer shadow
and no one knew.

Poor little ghost
who can't be free
until she captures
what she cannot see.

BLANK

Blind.
The slate stares back
with its words of routine,
but I can't see it.

Devoid.
So has my mind become,
numbers, dates, times –
where have they gone?

Remember.
Too hard to try,
little pieces of life
scattered, forgotten, or misplaced.

Blank.
A heart so hurting
that detachment feels safer
and so it goes.

ALONE

So, I'll be alone,
I'll just go it alone.

No one is there,
I might as well not care,
I'll just be alone.

There's no knocking at the door
to break the silence anymore,
I'll just go it alone.

All through the cold, dark nights,
an emptiness in the morning light,
I'll just be alone.

There's nothing else to lose,
I have only myself to confuse,
I'll just go it alone.

So, don't worry about me,
I'm okay can't you see?
I'll just be what I am,
alone.

THE COFFEE CUP

A shrine
left untouched
since Mark last stepped out
and shut the door
at the close of the
day.

And then he never returned.

The funeral
over, other lives resuming,
it was finally time
for me to visit this
sanctum.

I will greet his office for the first time.

A job transfer
brought us
to this faraway place.
Mark was happy and pleased with
his office containing the new ergonomic
furniture.

Now I must experience this workspace in its orphaned state.

A colleague
solemnly ushers
me inside. I sit at my husband's desk
and swivel the ergonomic
chair.

The computer screen is blank and dead.

Shadow So Dark

His books,
(technological, scientific, chemical)
line the shelves. I could never
comprehend their language, though
I loved the man who
understood.

The atmosphere speaks of study and creative energy.

A mug
sits forlornly
on the desk top. Inside this cup
a remnant of stale coffee
remains.

On the rim, a subtle stain marks the spot where he sipped.

This treasure
is what I latch onto.
It's as if his essence still lingers
because he left
an imprint to prove his
existence.

Colleagues arrive offering introductions and condolences.

Each member
of his team I invite
to select a book to remember
him by. I sign each one on Mark's
behalf.

Later, I pack his office paraphernalia.

Vacant walls
stare at me as I survey
the bereft bookshelves, the deserted desk,
the ergonomic chair. I inhale deeply the air
in the space Mark once
occupied.

Then I walk away, clutching to my heart the coffee cup.

BRINGING FLOWERS

This hill top holds the shell
of a precious treasure
I surrendered to the earth.

Solidly signifying the spot
stands a stone naming
who lies beneath.

I gaze down at the granite,
at the flowers, at the mound,
searching for the meaning of it all.

It is not to be found here
on this grave site
in this beautiful cemetery.

This is only a place
of memorial to those who
are engraved on our hearts.

So, here I stand on this
plot of real-estate; it is not
what I had bargained for.

I look out over the valley
below and wonder how I will
survive my husband's absence.

I pray for God's help
to endure the encroaching
emptiness that awaits me.

And, I will keep coming back
to this burial ground, bringing bouquets
to match the ever-shifting seasons.

Now, I will be the one
expressing my love by
bringing flowers.

THE LAND OF MY GRIEF

This is not what we came here for,
this Grief.

This is where we had hoped to transfer
our castles in the air to
a firm foundation
on the ground.

Instead, a nightmare came lurking
near our doorstep, and its darkness
curled around us like a
phantom that
would entrap.

Without a chance, Mark succumbed
to the mistakes the doctors made.

A blur of the unimaginable
and the inexcusable
smeared the days
together.

Though the sun shone in blue skies,
I could not acknowledge it.

The hospital became my world;
medical terminology and test results
were the drugs I craved.

But, ultimately Death rose up
and stood insurmountable,
casting with boldness
its shadow so dark.

Now I pay homage
to a grave site.

How could this be so soon
after moving to what has now become
the land of my grief?

Genesis 41:52

DELUGE & DESERT THUNDER & ICE

DESERTED ISLAND

uninhabited
    now that my beloved is
                      gone

deserted
    a drum without its
                      drummer

beating
    like a hand clapping
                      air

empty
    a shattered shell tossed
                      aside

heart
    an island lone and
                      still

RESIDUE

Inside
my heart a
vacuum dwells
like a plague. I have
lost something but I
cannot comprehend its
abstraction. For a sphere
of residency draws me in
and I am caught between
the past and the present.
I become a prisoner in a
nameless jail where I recall
neither home nor country.
I claim no recognition of
my own countenance. It's
as if a **bullet** has pierced
my soul, and as it exits,
steals a relic of residue
from the essence of who I am.

NEVER AGAIN

In my state of remembering
and longing
I find myself wedged
between two words
that have seized me
against my will.

The lonesomeness of
"never"
and the expectancy of
"again"
have collided
and refabricated my
reality.

Never again can I check
the "married" box on forms,
for I must submit to
"widow" as my label.

My wedding ring
adheres stubbornly
to its rightful place.
The dreaded unadornment
threatens to further
bereave me.

Roses will never again
arrive at my doorstep to announce
our many years of wedded
bliss and blunder.

Where are the dirty clothes
hastily thrown across the chair?
How small are the loads
of laundry now.
I never thought I would so miss
ironing his attire.

Where are the stacks
of important papers and books
he would leave in every
nook and cranny
of the house?

Sports will never again dominate
the television screen
in our home.
Nor is the computer
computing quite as much.

Never again will his
special Saturday breakfasts
greet us on those mornings.
Coffee for two
has been reduced
to just one.

His alarm clock will never again
annoy us weekday mornings.
Reasons to wake up so early
Are rather few these days.

His wing chair
remains empty and underused.
For who can fit into it
as perfectly as he could?

 Desert & Deluge, Thunder & Ice

Our king-sized bed seems to have
expanded somehow.
Every night I get lost as I search
for him in my sleep.

The big white robe
he wore every morning
now drapes across
the bed where he slept
every night.

Sometimes I slide my feet
into his shoes
and my arms into
the sleeves of his jacket,
hoping to feel a sense of him.

The insurance policies
classify me as the
"surviving spouse".
I'm not so sure that's
what I am doing.

I only know that
I live with an absence
I cannot embrace
and I contemplate
a future that whispers to me
day after day the words,
"never again".

NOT EVER!

So, it's over
and I have to accept it.
You won't ever walk
through that door again.

You won't ever
call my name,
or hold my hand,
or smile at me.

It's so over
and I can do nothing
about it.

Never
will I laugh at
your jokes
or cry on your
shoulder.

You are gone
and I can't
bring you back.

And I hate
the grave that
separates us.

For you
can never return
to me.

THE DOWNWARD GROOVE

Spiraling
without braking
downward
like a sinking prison
with no way
out

This is where
the mind
and heart
clasp hands
exchanging temperatures
each becoming the
enemy

Pursuing
without pausing
darkness
like a consuming cancer
with no known
cure

This is why
the thoughts
and beliefs
join forces
strangling facts
each destroying all
reason

Finding
without looking
emptiness
like a heavy shadow
with no possible
relief

This is how
the lies
and hurts
become partners
each entrapping the
other

WAVES

The eyes display
storms that enrage
the soul or golden rays
that warm the heart.

When tragedy
trespasses, the heart is
wrenched so violently
that denial tries to soothe.

As time plods by
the rainbow of emotions
continues to ride
the waves.

NO LONGER

The sorrow is profound
as is the silence.

His voice no longer echoes in my mind,
for it has been too long since he last
so playfully spoke my name.

I no longer have his hand to hold.
His arms are not there
to reach out and enfold me
into his warmth.

There is an empty place
where once he stood.
No longer is there the pleasure
of his presence
to look forward to.

Aloneness drapes me
like a chilling dew.
Wherever I go
I am unaccompanied.

I wait in vain
for the phone calls I used
to get from him
when we were apart.
How hushed is the
phone now.

He is no longer here
to pick up after.
There is no need to
wonder when he will
"get around to it."

I am forgetting how
to share and cooperate.
The art of compromise seems
not so necessary
anymore.

Discussions and debates
have dissipated in
our household –
it's not that exciting
to talk with oneself.
Why further emphasize one's
solitary circumstance?

I grasp for anything
of his that retains his
essence . . . for company.
But, it doesn't really
do the trick.

The thought of forgetting
the sound of his voice
and the silliness of his laughter
strikes terror in my soul.

To contemplate letting go
translates into a
nightmare
I cannot endure.

Every night I pray for
dreams of him.
But dreams are never
enough and in the morning
my heart aches
all the more.

"Why?" I cry out.
"Why, God, must I live
without him?"

"Did you think I do not
need him anymore?"

To be strong is too tiring
and hanging onto hope
wearies me.
Perseverance is such
a heavy burden.

My identity is nothing more
than a limping shadow.
A part of me has been
cruelly ripped away.

To live without him
is to die a daily death.
To look forward to the future
is to long desperately
for the past.

Remorse chases me down
from every direction.
I feel trapped by
the accusations of my mind.

So often I took him
for granted. I suffocate
from the regret
that rings throughout
my soul.

Is there any escape
from this mirage of madness?
Is there any relief
from the horror in my heart?

Or am I now left to merely
peer at the world
as if through a clouded window
and shuffle about in circles
as I grieve?

WOE

A heavy badge
upon the chest
pressing down on the heart
to crush it

A gauzy veil
over the eyes
masking a pain-spilled gaze
to hide it

A leaden chain
around the soul
choking out all the hope
to mute it

A sharpened knife
into the mind
slicing up each new thought
to thwart it

A somber cloud
above the world
blocking light from the sky
to grieve it

OUT OF ORDER

Don't hope for fire
or expect an ember,
glowing.

Don't listen for music
or even a gentle hum.

Don't wait for laughter
when smiling is a challenge.

Don't look for eyes with sparkles
or think you'll ever see
the ghost of a glimmer.

Because this heart is

OUT OF ORDER!

Note: an overhaul has not been
scheduled.

PRETTY THINGS

Things.
 Pretty things
 to surround myself with.

Jewelry,
books, clothes,
accessories, artwork.

Such company I keep.

But,
they are
no remedy for sorrow.

Nor
 can they
 enfold me in comfy hugs.

And
 they can't
 outshine a radiant smile.

Nor
 can they
 charm me with amusing anecdotes.

Nothing
can replace
a husband who has died.

So,
 I am
 now encompassed by anything lovely.

Yet,
 I am
 surrounded by everything empty.

Things.
 Pretty things
 decorating my loneliness.

A CLOSET FULL OF RAGS

I open the closet door
and look inside . . .
A solemn soliloquy
confronts me.

For before me hang
the clothes that once
attired the broad shoulders
and tall frame of my husband.

There is no one now
to give substance to the
idle apparel that has been
left behind without warning.

I take one of his shirts
off the hanger
and slide my arm into the sleeve
pretending he is holding me.

I put my feet into
his shoes, wishing he were here
to wear them and walk
alongside me.

I grab his robe and
hug it tightly, remembering
how warm and cuddly he was
to snuggle up against.

I realize, suddenly, that
these ties and shirts and
slacks and belts have lost
their purpose and their pride.

So, I close the closet door; but
I cannot shut away forever the mourning
of a wardrobe missing
its master.

It isn't the clothes that make
the man, of course. For
without the man, such raiment
is nothing but lifeless rags.

I flee this unintended altar,
knowing that however many times
I return to forage for his presence,
I will find only a lingering essence.

I cannot fill his shoes, nor can anyone
else. And so I am mocked
every time I review these
inert reminders.

They shout at me over and over
as they hang listlessly and lonely,
"He is not here! He is not here!
Nor will he ever be!"

Why do I torture myself?
Why do I sleep with his robe?
Why do I drown myself in his clothing?
Why do I keep hanging on to these remnants?

No hope can be found in a closet full
of dead possibilities; there can be no
expectation when all that greets you
is costume-wear for scarecrows.

Desert & Deluge, Thunder & Ice

As I pull his clothes off the
hangers to pack them away,
I feel as if I have lost him
all over again.

If only I could weave
my heart into the fabrics
he wore so well and make believe
we are together once again.

But, it would never be enough
and so I place the lid
on this box of quiet relics
and shut out the light of day.

When the deed is done
and my racing heart slows, I relocate
the naked hangers now stripped of purpose.
My tears rampage in protest.

Another time I shall return to
this closet and contemplate
the yawning vacuum where once
his apparel dwelled.

Until then I will leave
my widowed wardrobe to itself
and let it get accustomed
to the emptiness.

THE COLD PLACE

The suffocating grip
of pain is nearly impossible to
escape.

Sorrow surrounds me
and there is nowhere to shrink
from its presence.

Everywhere I turn, I face capture
as grief continues to constrict
and reality stings.

People look at me for a reaction.
They wonder how I am
holding up.

They seem amazed at my composure
and the lack of tears dripping
down my face.

What they do not recognize is
a heart paralyzed by an ache
too frightening to fathom.

They look into my eyes
and fail to see the anguish
of my severed soul.

I drift about in a mechanical
daze, doing what
I assume is expected of me.

The sun comes up, the sun goes down
and still it appears evident that I have
endured another day.

How do I survive when
I've lost the knight, the hero,
the truelove of my life?

How am I able to brush my
teeth and comb my hair
and shop at the store?

Where do I go when I'm
not really here as I meander through
the nights and the days?

The answer is fairly simple really –
I flee to that reservoir of nothingness:
the cold place.

It is a realm not reached by
those who have known only
sunshine and laughter.

Only the desperate know the way
and only they have the capacity
to interpret the map.

In this domain of invisible cold
my fears and my sorrows
freeze like statues.

They stand as solid reminders
of what I will encounter
when I go back.

The pandemic of pain that infiltrates
my heart is anesthetized
in the cold place.

Like a downy snow that blankets
the stark terrain of winter's realm,
so cloaks the cold place.

And while my senses are sensing
I am no longer aware of this
in the cold place.

There is freedom from thought and emotion,
from expectations and regret
in the cold place.

For it is only here in this palace
of silent emptiness that I know
I can rest in oblivious bliss.

But, only for a little while; for the line
between peace and delusion
is very fine indeed.

And the walls that keep the
rages at bay were not built
to last forever.

The clamor of life, however, refuses to refrain
and too soon I am awakened to address
its harassment.

I am hesitant to bestir
from my unencumbered existence
in the cold place.

For I have embraced the numbing
limbo of its cushioned barriers
that shield me from the outside world.

The sleeping solace of this place
has beguiled me into believing
I have peace.

It is not peace I have found, though,
but insulation from a traumatic loss.
Pain evasion is what first drove me here.

The time has come, at last, to look
at the monster of despair and acknowledge
its presence.

To be bold and stand before
the ravening stare of bereavement
and let its lacerations begin.

Mercy and Truth make a deal
and scheme to extract me from my
asylum of alleviation.

Degree by degree the intensity of
the freeze starts to lessen and
a thaw begins.

Everything around me is melting
and the frozen camouflage that once concealed me
now drenches me.

Suddenly, I realize that if I linger
I will drown; better to leave now
before puddles grow into rivers.

What had been a haven of false hope
has now mutated into a
personal prison.

I finally admit that
I must accept reality and face
what I could not face before.

At last, I waver no more and
relinquish the counterfeit comfort that
once was found in the cold place.

TEARS IN A BOTTLE

I have learned
to hold the tears back
and mimic a puppet's smile.

Inside, the heart
pretends to feel nothing,
while outside the eyes play the game.

There are other
kinds of teardrops besides those
that trace trails down sad faces.

Tears that never
stain the surface, yet
pollute the rivers of the soul.

Etchings encrusted with
salt linger briefly, but in deeper
regions they reign without end.

Such teardrops cannot
be wiped away with soft pastel tissues
or nicely pressed handkerchiefs.

No, such jewels
are meant for higher aims even
as sorrow sinks the grief-trussed spirit.

Hidden treasure troves
await the safe-keeping of spilled heartache,
though all seems wasted and lost.

One other knows
the brokenness that brings
the mourning dew upon bereaved landscapes.

He has seen
the weeping ocean of the soul
and the parched desert of the heart.

He has felt
the piercing prism of pain
and the belittling bruise of betrayal.

These unshed tears
fall in silence, yet there are ears
to hear what no one else has ever seen.

The untold stories
trapped inside each droplet of despair
are set free by He who redeems.

Catching our every
teardrop in a heavenly jar, He
releases into the mix every tear he never wept.

Holy and humble,
the weeping of all the ages is
collected and cherished by the One who loves.

He forgets not
the tragedies and treacheries, nor
the triumphs and mercies that touch us all.

He understands every
reason behind every façade and
every insanity behind every fact.

In a bottle,
He captures all our tears
and grieves with us our silent sorrows.

Psalm. 56:8

Desert & Deluge, Thunder & Ice

PULLING STRINGS

It's better this way
for a while,
this going through the motions
in numbing bliss
so merciful.

To be held up
for the moment
by invisible, strength-giving strings
pulled by unseen Hands.

One step, then two,
for the present
to get through the day
without falling apart.

Eventually, a gentle nudge
for a season
to safely unfold
and allow life to resume.

A slight, tender loosening
for a span,
string by shimmering string
releasing each nurturing embrace.

It's better this way
for all time
to walk along side
instead of pulling strings.

LET THE PAIN BEGIN!

In the coliseum of life,
a battle rages –
sport between two foes.

The game is ancient,
the rules eternity-etched,
the opponents well-known.

Two rivals face each other;
one looms larger
in this uneven match.

Pain ascends from grief,
its sword lifted high,
glinting sharp against the sky.

Behind a sturdy shield,
Denial stands firm, confident
in its numbing power.

For too long, Denial
has claimed victory,
its trophy becoming its idol.

But the sword of Pain
slices through Denial's shield,
shattering its anesthetizing ego.

The crowd roars in protest,
The queen rises from her throne,
the combatants clash in fury.

Grief finally has its day,
Denial sinks into the sand,
Sword slashes shield asunder.

And a new battle cry resounds,
piercing through the heart and soul,
"Let the pain begin!"

NOBLE SONG

Who can tell how deep
run the wounds of
a defeated heart?

Such a discovery may not
rise to the surface
for many a year.

But, a time will come
when the unshed tears
begin to fall

As the long suppressed
cries of devastation at last
are unleashed.

The simmering tempest will
finally make an appearance in all
its terrible splendor.

At that time the torrents
of rage and grief
will run rampant.

And the silent screams
of pain will shatter
the numbing stillness.

Then the great loss
that had so gripped the
heart with despair,

And had so plagued
the mind and soul
with denial,

Will reach out
to the skies and
embrace the truth.

The sound of truth encountering
tragedy will echo through
the halls of time.

And the ponderings of that
bruised and battered heart
will become its noble song.

HURTING

From the inner abyss of pain
to the outside void of denial
come the tears.

A ravage of hurt,
a desolation of soul
dripping,
leaving a trail of sorrow's
shrapnel
in their wake.

What sense can be made
from the cause
of this outpouring?

No consolation can
infiltrate
such a reservoir of misery.

Though each tear
may be counted
in this liquid symphony
as it cascades down the shattered faces
of the grief-stricken,

What does it matter
after all,
how many droplets
of anguish
are collected in
His bottle?

Why keep contained
these oceans, these rivers, these lakes
of saline-preserved sorrow?

Nonetheless,
the weeping continues its
purging baptism
over
the stolen happinesses,
the swept away hopes and dreams,
the lost loved ones –
all gone,
leaving only the imprints of
teardrops
to grace the loss.

FEEL

How do you articulate feelings
no words can express?

Are the tears that fall
from our eyes the songs of sorrows
stored in our souls?

Must we submit to the grief
that thrusts its cruel barbs
deep into our hearts?

Can we not shut the haunting
images away into the hidden
catacombs of our minds?

For there are certain sorrows
too painful to bear
and to acknowledge their reality
is to give yourself
over to a living
nightmare.

What do you do
when these marauders
prowling far beneath the
surface of your soul
clamor to get out?

Must you give free reign
to that which strives
to destroy you with its
incessant shrieking?

Is it possible to ignore
the internal torture
of unvented lament?

Desert & Deluge, Thunder & Ice

How deep is deep enough
to bury the memories of loss
before they can no longer
grip your heart in
their painful vise?

Why can't denial be a good thing?
Why must I feel this hazard
in my heart?

Why do I have to face
the unfaceable?

For to confront
that which
hurts me most
is to shatter my image of
survival.

But, I can no longer choke back
the cries in my throat.
They demand their
day!

Uncountable
are the murmurings
of melancholy my mind has squelched
as I insist on a stance of strength
no matter what.

But the cost has been too great.
My heart begins to wrench free
bellowing out its
protests.

An echo slaps back,
"Just feel!"

Desert & Deluge, Thunder & Ice

Yes, there is anger –
so be angry.
And wracking grief –
so grieve.
And the awful barrenness of
loneliness –
feel, feel the emptiness of it all.

And that triumphant torture
of letting go,
releasing the hopes, the plans, the dreams
and the sudden loss of love –
feel it deeply.

Feel, feel
the undeniable, persistent fact
that death has intruded,
it truly happened and
it cannot be undone.

Feel the fear, that quaking fear
of being a solitary someone
in the gatherings of society.
Feel the abundant
fruitlessness of it.

The flashback of witnessing
your loved one die one
desperate breath
at a time –
feel the inconsolable
devastation.

The daunting,
the overwhelming
elasticity of it all.
Let it snap you
out of your
stupor.

Feel the agony of
watching your children
deal with a loss they cannot
comprehend. Feel the helplessness.

Feel the waste of a life
cut short; feel the lost potential
and all the might-have-beens.

Feel it! Feel that deep, vast
unbridgeable chasm
of separation.

You must absorb it.
Embrace the loss; let
it be real to you.
Scream the screams,
mourn with might,
let the weeping torrents
drench you.

Feel every nerve ending
of every heartstring;
feel every shard of
every piece of
your heart.

Let it bleed!

Let it writhe!

Let it rupture!

FEEL!

ANGER

I raise my hand
up to the sky and I form a
fist.

I see the clouds
and they are scarlet,
deeply.

The wind turns
and twists like a serpent
searching for its
victim.

Lightning strikes
with venom, poisoning the earth
on which I
stand.

Thunder shatters
the void with the velocity of its
bellow.

Rain slashes
the air like wicked knives
with rapacious
teeth.

This storm,
in all its violence,
seethes and shrieks
hatefully.

I shake my fist
at it all, for my outrage reigns
unsurpassed over the skewered
skies.

The terror
of such fury is no
match for what is in my
heart.

O Anger,
you are not enough!

BLAME

Failures
come out of hiding
to lurk and haunt.

They know
I am weak, miserable
and open to accusation.

"You should have done things differently!"

Their slithering voices slide
into my consciousness and sink deeply
their teeth into my mind.

"If only you had chosen another path,"
they say as they distort
my thoughts and emotions.

"It's your fault,"
echoes the final indictment,
shattering my sanity.

Oh, to live with this kills me
from within,
for I have tasted the poison
of blame
and I know the strength
of its potency.

I bow my head in defeat,
beaten
by the desolation.

No matter
the mistakes made
by others,
I blame no one more
than I blame
myself.

Desert & Deluge, Thunder & Ice

APPRAISAL, PART ONE

Whole
no longer.
Just half of what once
was.

Like your best self has been irretrievably snapped off.

Valuable
no longer.
Just tarnished and torn
apart.

Like your soul has been severely diminished.

Useful
no longer.
Just empty and profoundly
futile.

Like your blood has been turned into water.

Remembered
no longer.
Just ignored and tossed
aside.

Like your heart has been dumped into the rubbish.

This then seems the way of it when
death sneaks in and snatches
the life of your loved one
away.

THE PRECIPICE

It is not mine to take, really,
when I think about it
with a clear mind.

Life was a gift, always,
from the start –
something I did not earn
or create –
it was simply given.

But like all gifts, cracks,
dents, wrinkles, fading –
all these come unwanted
and unasked for.

What to do when
brokenness comes, when
loss interrupts, when
pain presses down
hard and mean and constant.

What to do when
carrion comfort*
is all that remains
on the platter.

Let me untwist
these last strands*
and no longer be
so tethered.

Why must I keep it?
Why must I carry it?
Why must I remain under
it's spell?

But again, I am confronted
with the silhouette of its
being and its doing.

The denial I grasp for
slips through my feeble
fingers and then looks
back at me with mutiny
in its eyes.

For you cannot veto
the Truth.

The starkness of it
stands out strong.
It will not be ignored
no matter how cleverly
I try to do so.

I must value life
all the more because
of those who no longer can;
but when they could,
held it so dear.

This gift –
to be accepted,
but
never taken.

*"Carrion Comfort" by Gerard Manley Hopkins (1844-1889)

CALL IT LIKE IT IS

I shake my fist.
I don't know yet at what or whom,
but I raise my hand high
and grab what air I can
and squeeze with all my might.

The fuel to do this is
anger
and it has not
a pretty face.

To love someone
and watch them suffer
and die when it should not
have been
is a kind of death
all on its own.

Death meets death.
Only
one of them keeps
breathing
just so Torture can
stay alive.

And so
I shake my fist of fury
to declare the strangling
of my soul.

I let it wound and writhe
my heart;
otherwise,
I would not feel.

Oh, to come alive by
the rampage of wrath
is to walk on burning coals
without the sizzle of flesh.

Fierce fist-shaking
may murder the emptiness,
smothering the life out of
the nothing in one's hand,

But, it is a poor partner
for Grief, and can
no more quench the fire of rage
than a flaming torch.

My hardened fist
serves me no great gain after all,
for with it I can gather no answers
nor summon healing
to my heart.

It is merely a symbol
of a simmering hurt seeking
an elusive consolation.

Finally, I call it like it is:
anger is just anger –
it brings no glory and
justifies no end.

And though I raise my fist,
I must, in the end, fold my hands
and fall to my knees.

RELICS OF GRIEF

Tears,
plentiful or meager,
fall when
death empties our
world.

Weeping,
deluge or desert,
rains down
hurt, secret or
seen.

Mourning,
loud or quiet,
lets pain
achieve its true
goal.

Emotions,
free or enslaved,
find solace
as sorrow opens
up.

Tears,
now or later,
carry away
relics of unexpressed
grief.

IN THE HEAVENS OF MY HEART

In the heavens of my heart
vast treasuries reside
where memories of the one I love
abide ever so gently –

What heights of gladness were
found in his good presence;
what depths of passion
were revealed in his loving eyes!

Yet, in the hades of my soul
untold poverties lurk
where remembrances of the one I miss
irk ever so cruelly –

What depths of sorrow are
discovered in these dark oceans;
what heights of longing
are reached in these somber skies!

Whether heaven or hades
great turmoil reigns
where imaginings of the one I mourn
rule ever so keenly –

Oh, what heights of hurting are
spanned on this long journey;
what depths of anguish
are fathomed in his sudden demise!

AN ACCOUNTING

WEEDS
A Subterfuge

They grow, unwanted, amongst the beauty
and there is no rhyme or reason
to them.

They are unsightly, yet they are strong
and persistent, growing wherever
they can.

Stubbornly, their roots reach down deep
while outwardly their wily tendrils
smother all.

I wrestle with them frantically,
for such pestilence must
be expunged.

Overhead, dark clouds are looming,
black and boiling and full
of doubt.

What to do, what to do, what to do?
is the mantra that keeps thundering through
my thoughts.

And one by one, I extract the invaders
leaving the turf tattered
and torn.

But, I need answers to the dilemma
that has infiltrated my world
with disarray.

Like a weed that chokes the life
out of a well-tended plant, the
saboteur assaults.

For it twined its willful way
around the cherished stem
and squeezed.

Until, of a sudden, the breath
of life was snatched away and the flower began
to wilt.

How do you reverse the irreversible;
how do you turn back the hands
of time?

Is silence to be worn like a heavy
shroud that smothers the voices struggling to
be heard?

The weeds pile up into a scraggly mound,
leaving the flower bed increasingly free
from strangulation.

Reasons to remain silent
blow away like chaff before a
bustling breeze.

 *An Accounting*

The first sprouts of an idea begin
to shoot outward from the furrowed fields of
my mind.

If you become aware of an
impending danger, yet shout
no warning,

Would you not also share in
the guilt and the guile responsible for
harm done?

Over and over this question sears
itself into my soul, showing me
no sympathy.

My hands are stained with grime
and dirt has imbedded itself beneath
my fingernails.

Then the tears burst forth and rain down
unrepentantly upon the soil on which
I kneel,

Watering the ground
with the salty spoilage of
my discontent.

I stand up and gather together
this haphazard heap of
trespassers.

They are tossed away and remembered
no more. The havoc they had caused
has ceased.

In freedom the flowers can at last
grow gleefully and send forth their beauty and
their fragrance.

And I too will no longer succumb
to the stranglehold of uncertainty that entangled
my thoughts.

The land of my grief will not
become a haven for the malignancy of
a cover-up.

The truth shall flourish for all to see
and injustice will be uprooted
like weeds.

THE CHAMBER

Cavern
where secrets are kept
in the dark
in the deep
buried

Pain
digs its way out to
pierce the soul
pummel the heart
ravage

Escape
runs out of options
from the fear
from the dread
paralyzing

Denial
lasts only so long
through the day
through the night
numbing

Memory
hints of a presence
to be felt
to be heard
realized

Grief
wakes from its slumber
sees the broken
sees the lost
weeping

Open
the hidden door to
let in light
let in air
freedom

Cavern
no more a chamber
for the hurt
for the hate
restored

ACCOUNTABLE

A day comes when
you must stand up
and face
the wreckage you have left
in the wake of your walk.

We are all authors
of the tales we tell,
and actors
in the scenarios and seasons
we encounter along
the way.

For some, a legacy
of love and hope
gives testimony
to a collage of kindness
and nurturing goodwill.

There is no cleanup
then, following a life lived
so well.
A good account
has been given.

But, for others,
a trail of pain and grief
generously litters
the path they have tread.

Left behind are
the lives that have been shredded
by wrongs committed
and truth omitted.

And in cases
such as these, there is
a need
to hold the doctor
accountable.

Do no harm, right?

So, when a procedure
goes awry due to
gross negligence
and the patient
is irreversibly injured,
what accounting should
there be?

The door has been opened
to Death and in
an instant
a living human being
is living no more.

How can such injury as this
be rectified when
a life taken cannot be
returned?

Answers, facts, details . . .
are these not necessary for
an accounting?
Oh, the mistakes that can mutate
the histories of our lives!!

Though forgiveness is offered,
the desperate longing
for justice
still remains, an acknowledgement
of truth is needed.

How could it ever
be denied that it is
only honorable
to stand up and face
the consequences; that it is
only right to be held
accountable?

DEPOSITION

Interrogating
by shooting insidious bullets
at the heart and mind
of the grieving.

Attempting
to whittle away at
the cherished memories
of the one who was lost.

Delving
into unspeakable pain,
forcing verbal answers
from numb witnesses.

Probing
for non-existent discrepancies
in a harrowing narrative
of stunning bereavement.

Punishing
the shell-shocked survivors
for pursuing truth
and exposing misdeeds.

Devaluing
the worth of a man
in order to renege
on restitution.

Pursuing
the justice seekers
like criminals, insensitive
to their trauma.

Scheming
to shield the guilty
from penalty or penance
by belittling the injury.

Denying
liability or blame
for cutting short a life that
had shone so bright.

ARBITRATION

A glorified farce
staged to pretend that a miserly
concession can smooth over
malpractice.

In one room,
the plaintiffs strive
to unshackle the
stifled truth.

In the other room,
the defendants disdain
all harm done in order to better
protect their assets.

In between
the mediator glides
from one room to the other,
presenting offers and rebuffs.

Hopefulness reassembles
into righteous anger as
representatives for the defense
offer surface skimmings –

Injurious insults
placed on corroded trays
meant to invalidate
the plaintiffs' suffering and pain.

After long days toiling
in the fields of arbitration,
all that has been achieved
is an exhausted exasperation.

The counsel for the defense
strides away with no sweat
on their brows or apparent
stirrings in their hearts.

While the plaintiffs sit
silently in stunned disbelief
as a shivering slices
into their souls.

The horizon did not
brighten on such days as these
when wrongs were left unfettered
and indemnity was put on ice.

VALUE

What is the value of a man?
Can you tell me?
Is it in how much he loves
his family, his friends, his God?

Is it found in the respect
he gives his country and
in the sacrifice he makes for its
its protection?

Or, could it be found in the laughter
he creates by telling funny stories, or singing
silly songs, or acting goofy, or talking
in funny voices and made-up languages?

Maybe his value is found in working hard,
honoring his employer, in volunteering,
or perhaps in the teaching
of a Sunday school class.

Could his value be measured by the blueness
of his eyes, or by the brilliance of his smile,
or even by the firmness of his handshake or
by the comfort given by his grizzly bear hugs?

Do his kisses count in the calculation?
Can the flowers and the cards he gives, or the
love poems and romantic letters he writes be
added to the equation of how much he is worth?

Tell me, how valuable is this man
I love, this man who never ceased putting
up with my many moods, this man who always
rescued me, this man who stood tall for me?

 *An Accounting*

What is the price for prayers prayed and
patience practiced, for listening to a poured out
heart, and for the giving of himself for
the good of others?

Well, I know the answer and it is this:

He is worth as much as the beauty
of sunsets and the color of rainbows;
as much as the majesty of mountains
and the splendor of the oceans.

He is worth every beat of my heart
and every breath I take. And he is worth
all the pain and all the sorrow that
wrenches my soul as I grieve for him.

That is the value of this man!

REVENGE

In his hands
harm came
and it was permanent.

We put our trust
in this doctor
and in his assurances.

But they were just ... empty words.

Death to the brain came first.
A week later
the body complied.

Gone ... Over ... Finished

One mistake
led to another and another
until the staggering end.

And then came the scourge of If only's ...
night and day and
in between.

Destructive grief ruled the heart –
a bitter pathway through
the soul.

It was a not so great escape.

Vengeance wreaked havoc
with my convoluted
thoughts.

There had to be a better way
to navigate
this territory of toxicity.

Then, an inkling
of grace interceded
and my heart tried to listen.

The whisper took wing
and metamorphosed into mercy
before flying straight into my soul.

Bursting like a kaleidoscope,
a new design coalesced
out of the fragments of my heart.

Revenge . . . revised.

So I embraced this
retaliation
and planned my strategy.

One by one
the words marched in formation
as I gave them their weapons.

Not empty, but loaded.

The "enemy" didn't see it coming:

Ambushed
by a prayer
of blessing and forgiveness.

At last,
I found a way to survive
the battle.

For only in this way
could God accept
my revenge.

REFUGE & RESCUE

PRAYER

Hidden

inside my heart
are wordless

Pleas

for help and
comfort cried in

Silence

heard only by
a listening

God

sees the invisible
hears the

Unspoken

because a heartquake
goes beyond

Language

cannot capture the
depth of

Sorrow

paints with colors
doleful and

Deep

is the anguish
of the

Soul

where the fractures
of the heart ever

Echo

because such petitions
search for

Expression

in wordless chanting
never before

Heard

only by One
who captures

Prayer

ignited by faith
longing for

Rescue

given with mercy and
a love never

Hidden

GOD IN THE HURT

I wonder . . .
who is with me in the hurt?
Or do I walk alone?

I am solitary,
with a torment deep inside
that attempts to devour
my heart with pain
unspeakable.

"No," I choke,
"I refuse this path!"
Yet there it is stretching out before me.

I try
to retreat, but
the way is barred
by the present tense,
and the past turns its back.

My feet
are heavy with the muck
of fear and doubt.

I hate
what I face
as a churning fog looms ahead,
threatening
to engulf me
with
its calculating camouflage.

"Who is there
to fight for me and
slay the hurt I dread?"

No answer
comes that I can hear
as I force myself to
take one step forward
on this unwelcomed journey.

My soul
screams bitterly
as a cloud of sorrow
hovers heavily over me.

Then, a sudden shifting
of this shadow, slight though it be,
steps back from me,
and I am gently nudged
forward.

I have
no choice now, unless
it is to fold up
and give in to
despair.

I stumble
from the searing intensity of
what I believe to be
more than I can endure.
"Such loss
cannot be borne,"
I cry.

A whisper
brushes up against me,
and like snowfall,
lingers
on my shoulders.

The ache
does not vanish, but
spreads out over the landscape
of another heart, another spirit,
thinning
the weariness of it all.

I know,
at last, that this anguish
I so abhor
is accepted readily
by my Companion.

A shared
ownership of heartache
exists
between me and the One
who silently, invisibly
walks alongside me
in the valley.

He steps
into my grief, not willing
for me to
go it alone.

He holds
my hurt, allowing
its ferocity
to lacerate His Hands.

Now we
both carry the cross
of heartbreak and sorrow,
because
we dared to love.

And so
I have my answer –
honest and unyielding:
Not to remove
the prism of pain, but
to share in the
suffering
of it.

PUNISHMENT SYNDROME, *PART ONE*

Clashing thoughts
shove up against each other
and collapse upon themselves
only to rise up
and attack again.

The force
of their power
sinks the beaten heart
and pours dread
deep into the pockets of the mind.

A frantic
desperation silently seeps
through the cracks
of a shell-shocked,
and battle-weary soul.

"You deserve
this", they screech and scream.
"It's all your fault",
continues the staccato chant,
like poisoned arrows piercing the brain.

Such weaponry
of words rage and wage
a war of accusations
against a weakened prey.

The assault
twists the truth and taunts
with lies, brandishing a banner
boldly spelling PUNISHMENT.

No reasons
are offered, nor are terms
of surrender mapped out,
just the idea bullied
forward to hurt and depress.

"But why?"
cries the agonized,
as a growing despair attempts
to swallow all hope

"Is there
no antidote; is there no defense?"
drones the guilt-ridden griever,
who is about to succumb
to the brain wash.

PUNISHMENT SYNDROME, *PART TWO*

Silence
claims the ensuing moments,
denying the sway of pervasive,
guilt-inducing verbiage
from further abuse.

The punishing
thoughts are captured
one by one and deflated,
deemed null and void
by incoming evidence.

A surrounding
of comfort from the caring
and the kind shines forth
like a shield emblazoned
with gold and fire.

The rescue
succeeds due to prayers
lifted for one
who is stumbling
through a battlefield of lies.

So Hope
conquers the pawns of despair
and Truth, in all its mercy
defeats deception and its tyranny
at last.

RUNNING

Running
away from, maybe
toward something, don't know
but
running anyway.

Trying
to pretend, doesn't work
to deny what's real, a waste
and
it's another day.

Chasing
off feelings, they return
full force, so weary
for
they are here to stay.

Crying
acrid tears, drenched
words pour out, He listens
to
the grieving prayers I pray.

Hoping
to cheat pain, it hits
back harder, I discover
this
truth will finally have its say.

Running
into The Arms, wide open
to catch me, knowing
that
He will love me all the way.

Isaiah 40:11
Psalm 34:18

Refuge & Rescue

BREAK THROUGH

Barricade,
blocking my path
keeping me cold,
bereft.

Hammer,
nailing my heart
beginning a slow
theft.

Chisel,
chipping my soul
exposing a jagged
cleft.

Infiltrator,
permeating my mind
invading with skill,
deft.

Balm,
soothing my pain
healing what is
left.

LIKE A THIEF

I sense
The Lord chipping away
at the wall of resolve
I have built
in order to keep myself
imprisoned by the punishment
I believe I deserve.

"Who are you
that you take so much
upon yourself?"
He says.

"Did you give birth
to Time?

"Do you lift up the sun
in the morning
or hang the stars and the moon
at night?

"Have you designed the plans
and prepared the purposes
for all who walk
upon the face of the earth?

"So, therefore, you have no authority
to cast wide the net of blame,
nor do you have the right
to crawl beneath
its weight.

"For it is I, God Almighty,
who allows and appoints –
nothing is beyond my control;
my power cannot be
diminished.

"Though my ways may not
be understood,
I establish the span of life
and I ordain the moment
of its conclusion.

"Throughout it all
My Love enfolds,
My Grace carries,
My Mercy covers.

"Blame has no place
in your heart,
and so, like a thief,
I take it from your possession
and dismantle its
dominion."

Job 38: 12, 17-18

KEEPING MY HEART

Break
shatter completely
I let it go

Tear
shred savagely
I do not care

Misplace
forget intentionally
I refuse to search

Neglect
ignore coldly
I turn my back

Discard
toss callously
I cast it off

❦

Mend
rebuild carefully
He takes His time

Bind
restore gently
He repairs the rift

Find
recover joyfully
He embraces my soul

Nourish
loves deeply
He returns me home

Reclaim
shelter securely
He keeps my heart

Refuge & Rescue

RELEASED

You think
no one sees you
in the dusk
of your abysmal despair.

You feel
alone with your pain
in the grip
of an overwhelming grief.

You believe
you are a prisoner
in the cage
of your consuming outcry.

You realize
you have put yourself
in the path
of a raging pretender.

You hope
there is an escape
from the throes
of this entangling turmoil.

And then . . .

He sees
deep into your soul.
With His Dawn
He embraces your despair.

He carries
you and your pain.
With His Grace
He takes upon Himself your grief.

He frees
you from your prison.
With His Care
He vanquishes your outcry.

He removes
you from destruction.
With His Plan
He defeats the pretender.

He saves
you from entrapment.
With His Truth
He untangles the turmoil.

TIME

The Time
I've not waited for
has come.

It did not march,
but crept.

And until I acknowledged it,
my soul was in its debt.

But Time
could not be ignored,
nor stopped.

It did not shout
or cry.

For until I gave up my pleading
I'd be trapped by the question, "Why?"

Yes, Time
knew the track it had
to take.

It would not change
or bend.

And until I learned acceptance
my heart would never mend.

So Time
won the game we played
at last.

It did not gloat
or jeer.

And when I followed its leading
I ceased to live in fear.

THE LOUDEST THING

Sometimes
to be quiet
is
the loudest thing
you can
say.

For
who can put
words
to the tune
of a
memory,

Or,
the tremor of
pain,
or the piercing
of the
heart?

What
name does sorrow
call
when the soul
is mute
inside?

How
can one describe
despair
when the eyes
see only
darkness?

Is
there any fitting
eulogy
for the death
of a
dream?

Only
the color of
truth
gives hope to
those who
hurt.

Often
the music of
joy
is heard only
by the
spirit.

Love
sings in the
heart
a song which
is simply
felt.

Action
need not speak
when
comfort walks beside
one who
weeps.

Words
left unspoken are
often
the loudest thing
you can
say.

CLING

I look into my fractured heart
for the missing slivers,
but while searching
I trip and fall.

I question whether I will
find anything left unbroken
upon this tormented
terrain.

Surveying the vista of
writhing wretchedness
I shrink back, afraid
of its venom.

I retreat, hoping to find
refuge from the pain
that threatens to rise up
over the horizon.

But there is nowhere to hide
and I stand exposed to
the elements
swarming about me.

I shrink down into myself seeking
oblivion; instead I sense a
whisper swirl around me
like a soft mist.

"Walk with me," I hear.
So I watch and wait, wondering
who would dare come near
me in this desolation.

Then His Presence clears the air,
and in compassion He reaches
out and offers me a Hope
to cling to.

Psalm 46:1
Psalm 103:8
Isaiah 40:31
Lamentations 3:22
James 5:11

FOR US

Suddenly,
a new identity
knocks me over and
takes ownership.

Widow,
it is called.

And my children
are taken hostage
by the caption,
"Fatherless".

It is the Day of Minuses.

When a husband's voice,
a father's laugh,
are no more.

When his presence, always
there to affirm,
to love and protect,
is gone.

And it is final.

But God
reminds us
that He is still here
holding us up,
ever showing us how
to navigate
the wide-open sorrow
filled to the brim
with Empty.

Because
without this husband,
this father,
the horizon before us
looms vast in its
vacancy.

With each minute, each hour; however,
God paves our path with
Mercy.

During each day
He pours Himself
into the care of us, and
throughout the impending
nights of slumber
or sleeplessness,
He becomes our shield
against the fears that flourish
in the dark.

Provision greets us
at every corner
and keeps us company,
becoming a mosaic
of many colored
kindnesses.

Rescue and Refuge,
our side-kick comrades,
follow us everywhere.

Looking over us and sheltering
us in the circle of His Arms,
God helps us and
defends us.

Though now acquainted
with the pangs of mourning,
we stand with strength
because God is for us
and He is true.

Deuteronomy 10:18
Psalm 68:5
Romans 8:31

FISTFUL

I always thought another day
would be best
for the loosening
of my grip,
one white-knuckled finger
at a time.

Then, with my palms open
to the expanse,
I would release my hold
on regrets,
on what once was,
on a love six feet under.

But a self-shrinking ghoul
kept seizing my soul,
and the fear of
living without the pretense
of Mark's presence
overcame my sanity.

Eventually I discover, while
so clutched within
the fist of denial,
that my heart is that fist.
Instead of life-giving,
it has served to defeat me.

After waking up from this daze,
a day comes when I can
look back and see,
not a letting go, but
a slow and steady
giving over.

Dreams, hopes, sorrows, and
the pain of
missing my husband
are set free
to find refuge
in better Hands.

And this One to whom
I entrust all
that I am
and all that I hope for,
graciously accepts
these treasures.

With mercy in His Fingertips,
He transforms the temporal
into the eternal, never to be forgotten.
I learn that to let go
is to gain
what is true.

HOPE RECLAIMED

SOLITAIRE, I THOUGHT

I thought
I would have to go through all of this
alone.

That somehow
I would have to pick up all the pieces
by myself.

It seemed
I would have to find my way around
and learn to bear my burdens
on my own.

I would need to be brave and strong
to endure
the painful loss while keeping
my grief contained.

I thought
I would have to let go and move on
alone.

That somehow
I would have to learn to make a new life
by myself.

This is what I thought,
but it is not what I discovered.

For I discovered
Someone going through all of this
with me.

That somehow
He picked up all the pieces
Himself.

He walked ahead
and showed me the way to go
while carrying my burdens
on His own.

He gave me courage
and strengthened me, understanding
my pain and validating
my loss.

I discovered
Someone instilling hope, and taking that next step
with me.

That somehow
He would make all of life new
Himself.

This is what I discovered,
despite what I had thought.

HOPE

I question the purpose of
sorrow, I protest the severity
of pain; yet everywhere I turn
I am accosted by these
mutations of mourning.

An answer hovers over me.
I can sense it trying
gently to break through the
curdled clouding
of my grief.

Gradually, a glimmer
of mercy pierces the gloom
and sparkles on the surface
of my soul.

A radiance begins to
shine inward and it is Grace.
Then comes a Love that
illuminates all the hiding places
where Despair had been lurking.

Try as I might to shrink
from the Source of this aura,
I cannot.

God's searchlight has found me
and reveals every crevice
and corner from which
I tried to lose myself.

A promise of healing
is bestowed upon me.
Yet, I am warned
that my heart
will never be
the same.

Hope Reclaimed

For there is no turning
back to what might
have been.

The one for whom
my heart beat
abides now in an eternal
Home of Joy
unlike any he has
ever known.

I must now face
the truth of a
tomorrow framed
with sorrow.

And I must carry on
and walk in the light of
a promise that will one day
be fulfilled.

So, I live
with the prayer
of honoring the God
of my hope.

No longer
lamenting my loss
for always, but
remembering with gladness
the man I love
who will never leave
my heart.

REGRETS

It's too late
to make up for
lost time.

Too late
to be a better wife,
a kinder friend,
less grumpy,
more patient.

My reward:
to be pushed around
by regrets –
such bad company
I keep.

I want to bury myself;
after all,
my better half
is already
buried.

To redeem myself
I think back
to those moments
that mattered,
that lifted life up
in beauty.

To look closely
at the one
I loved dearly,
studying the way
he walked,
never forgetting
the deep blue
of his eyes
or the sweeping range
of his smile.

To remember
every nuance of
his being:
his voice, his laughter,
his frown
and his frame.

My hand nestled in his
was a heavenly thing;
the warmth of his hugs
a great wonder.

To dance for no reason,
singing nonsensical songs –
these treasures
proved the day was
not wasted.

To catch tears
and give up grudges,
to knit our souls
together with
prayer.

Such memories
bring a warmth into my heart
and embrace my soul
with healing.

Regrets,
though painful,
suddenly turn into
stepping stones toward
a higher cause:

To shun
the selfish whims
that clutter my attempts
to love
and to welcome the
unseen radiance
that resides within
those little gifts
I forget to
receive.

GRIEVE

When clouds hide the sun
and the land is shrouded in shadow,

When the fire has flickered out
and the embers have grown cold,

When the petals of the rose
have wilted and fluttered to the ground,
grieve.

When the heart is broken
and the dreams have limped away,

When the casket is lowered into
the depths of the earth,

When that place at the table
glares back bleak and vacant,
grieve.

And when the final epitaph
is at last engraved in stone,

When the silence is deafening
and his absence cannot be denied,

When hope seems lost forever
and the warmth of love has faded,
grieve.

When the future cruelly taunts
with a promise of loneliness,

When there is no one to walk beside
and no hand to hold,

When the time has come to
let go and face the land of the living,
grieve.

And when grief begins to
loosen its grip upon your heart,
let it go.

APPRAISAL, Part Two

"Not so!"
says God, the Father, who
desires mercy for the fatherless
and the widow.

"For I see
the depth of your sorrow
and I have heard
the lament of your heart.

"Only I
can catch the tears
that stream from your soul
in the palms of my Hands.

"It is I
who can embrace
your emptiness and make
you whole again.

"I will
polish you with
my love, for you
are highly valued.

"It is
through your weakness that
my strength empowers,
helping you to overcome.

"You are
cherished beyond all
measure and your name
is written on My Heart.

"This is the way of it, for
my gift of eternal life proves
your worth to me."

Hope Reclaimed

LETTING GO

Letting go
is like a silent
killing of the
heart –

A final
farewell to a long
remembered dream, a never
forsaken love.

I watch
the fluttering away
of a
kindred spirit.

My soul
no longer soars
because my flight has
been diverted.

To hang on
is to fill my days with a
pseudo existence which leaves
me drained.

In truth,
I am merely nurturing
an illusion that can never
become real.

A fantasy
such as this will flounder
when the sparkle of wishful thinking
flickers out.

Grasping for
what is already lost frays
my every fiber, yet still
I grasp.

Peace never
comes to me when
my stranglehold
remains steadfast.

Weaker grows
my grip, however,
as my will to
persevere diminishes.

Darkness cloaks
me like a heavy frost
that slowly seeps into my
every pore.

I succumb
to a sleepless slumber,
an enslavement to the numbing of
my mind.

My every
turning finds me trapped between
what once was and what might
have been.

Looking back
inflicts as much
pain as
looking forward.

Hope Reclaimed

Past and Future
skillfully weave
about me a
perilous web.

The Present
is just a place to dwell
while I pretend my
life away.

I learn
to ignore the grief
that gnaws through
my heart.

I disregard
the rising wave of unwept tears
that batter against the dam of
my denial.

The grave
stares blankly back at me
as I return again and again
to remember.

I fall
repeatedly on the gravel
of despair until the skin of my resolve
is shredded.

When finally
I come to the end of myself,
I discover there is nowhere left
to cling.

Time stretches
out before me like a ravenous monstrosity,
the appetite of which cannot
be appeased.

I begin
to discover that what I have been
clutching so tightly has already
slipped away.

As I
ever so cautiously
unfold my fists, I see an
amazing thing:

Nothing.

I held
onto this vacancy for so long
that I forgot what living
was for.

I realize
in that moment of awakening
something I never could
have believed:

Hanging on
to a hollow reality
hobbles the velocity of
my heart.

To give
thanks for the gift I had
in Mark requires
open hands.

And only
in letting go
can my heart's love
prove true.

 *Hope Reclaimed*

NOT ANYMORE

I will not harbor
bitterness
or blame
anymore.

I will leave them
in the shadows
from which they came.

Nor will I carry
resentment
or rage
for

I will dump them
in the quagmire
where they
belong.

I will not nurture
fretfulness
or fear
anymore.

Instead, I will
toss them in the
junkyard
where they may
decompose.

I will not self-destruct
anymore!

COMFORT

At first, when pandemonium prevails,
the days are too difficult to decipher –
you are weak, your hands are clinched, yet empty.

Robotically, you do what you must,
for there is no other way to manage life
when death intrudes so boldly.

Though the minutes take you further from sudden shock,
they also take you closer to the sure reality of your loss,
opening a door to every emotion the heart has ever known.

In awe, you wake in the morning disbelieving what has happened,
while at night, you go to bed swamped in despair,
concealing yourself in slumber, hoping no dreams interfere.

Through the days, your eyes do not see
and your ears do not hear—all is blurred and muffled,
all seems hollow, trivial.

No answers come, no perfect words of comfort emerge
even though you are surrounded by well-wishers
and offers of help and company.

Nothing can reach you where you are,
trapped in a heart that is sequestered,
buried in a sorrow that is numbing and bleak.

Your prayers are one-worded and desperate –
"Help!" you cry. "Why?" you scream. Tears may fall
or stay hidden and dry; either way, there's no relief.

Equinox; Solstice – they continue their interplay while the world
barely blinks over your bereavement. But, you do not fault this
world, so full to the brim with its own sufferings.

 *Hope Reclaimed*

One day you are able to look back and see that
along this journey through the shadelands, friendships
beamed into the shadows, hands and feet lifted and supported.

You realize you never could have taken a single
faltering step had not someone been there either in
spirit or form, in card, letter, or call.

Through it all, blessings abounded, each one
orchestrated to accompany you, to befriend you, to
help you to endure, and to grasp, at last
the comfort of God.

Hope Reclaimed

TURN AROUND

Look over your shoulder
and turn around.

In so doing, you face what
you could not face before.

A sense of loss and a sense of gain
seem to be interchangeable.

The heart may be buffeted by
both hope and despair.

In going forward, there can be no
continual looking back.

For a journey commences by
heading toward a new horizon.

But, refusal to go on will result
in a sure stagnation.

And life will slowly turn into
an ever-empty existence.

Although sorrow may linger,
and pain might persist,

Endure by drawing strength from
the Father who blesses.

The dread of each dawning day
will begin to diminish,

While the dread of the night
gradually fades away.

New dreams will arise miraculously
from the rubble.

At last, you see color again
where once all seemed gray.

The grief that so engulfed your soul
loosens its grip.

For the one you loved
is not gone forever,

But, resides near the One Who Saves
for all time.

Until that longed-for moment
of true ever after,

Let go of what you cannot control
and turn around.

THE DARK GREY

On the brink
waiting for an answer,
we try to keep our balance
on this sheer, cold
precipice.

We hope for
justice to reach across
this chasm and bridge the
gulf between truth and
accountability.

For too long
sodden clouds of
uncertainty have hovered over
our lives, squelching our attempt to
shine light in dark places.

One phone call
will bring a decision to
our sobering pursuit of facts
so that we can extract good from
grave mistakes.

The ringing startles
as I answer and listen, my
breath held to hear the outcome:
shall there be a trial or
a settlement?

Oh at last
the end to a painful,
twisted journey has come;
a settlement and a difference
to be made for the benefit
of others.

The dark grey
is lifting, and a ray of
hope shines through, bringing
a song of Joy to shove
the clouds
away.

MOVING ON

They say a time will come
to move on
from sorrow.

That the pain of loss
will diminish
one day.

Though the hurt and harm
are not forgotten
nor denied,

Fragments of happiness hover near-by
waiting to be
assembled.

The scattered promises of the past
coalesce and reform,
instilling hope.

A new vision rises from
the poverty of
demolished dreams.

Sorrow's place in the heart
gives way to
a timid smile.

Not because the loss is less,
for love will
always remain,

But because moving on proves
our loved one's life
was not lived in vain.

 *Hope Reclaimed*

NO BROKEN TOMORROW

Dreams
    Love
        Wealth
            Health
can be lost
    or broken
        or stolen.

Sometimes, there is no defense;
    sometimes there is.

However it goes,
    or wherever,
it is not always the end,
and the finish line
    may still be
        way up ahead.

Beginnings
    have to come from
        somewhere;

and somewhere is often
    in the valleys
        of our lives.

Be there, then.
    Take a step
        toward that horizon
            you've never seen before.

It has always been there
    veiled behind
        what we thought was
            ours to keep.

Hope Reclaimed

Now, we have discovered
 that all we can do
  is borrow for a time
   a heart's desire,
    a childish wish,
     a hoped-for prize,
      a noble goal.

  Forever
   is not promised
    for the earthbound
     treasures we seek.

But, we weep all the same
when they filter through
   our fingers like
    sand through a sieve.

What, then, is everlasting?

What can we hold on to?

  Faith in the Son
   and treasure
    secured through His love.

  How Eternity
   welcomes
    such as these!

Hand in hand,
　　saved with the Savior,
　　　　to never look back
　　because before us

is no broken tomorrow,
　　but fulfilled hope
　　　　and an everlasting
　　　　　　celebration of life
　　　　　　　　in abundance.

GRATITUDE

THE WORK OF THEIR HANDS

Many doctors and specialists
gave all they had
to do all they could
to rescue Mark
from oblivion.

Empathetic and proficient,
these doctors were always
quick to keep us informed
and updated on
Mark's condition.

Though, ultimately,
there was nothing they could do
to resuscitate my husband,
they stood by us and
grieved with us.

May God bless
the work of their hands,
guiding them
and strengthening them
to heal others.

THE NURSES

Like salve
on a wound
they soothe and protect,
working ceaselessly
to give comfort
and compassion
and encouragement.

Like a cool cloth
on a fevered head
they bring relief and calm,
tending tirelessly
to insure recuperation
and restoration
and revival.

With thanks
I will extol
their kindnesses and care,
never forgetting
their skill
and support
and sympathy.

BECAUSE OF YOU

You offered sanctuary
to me
when I knew not where
to go.

In the darkest hours
of my days
your compassion brought light
to my soul.

I was a stranger
to you all,
yet you welcomed me and offered
your friendship.

You enfolded me
in your prayers
and you comforted me
in my grief.

With grace, you listened
to my heart
as it shattered into a
thousand pieces.

With gentleness you searched
for those pieces
and helped me gather them together in
a safe place.

When I could not face
another day,
you showed up and we faced
the day together.

When my hope faltered and
grew dim,
you lent me the radiance of
your hope.

Because of you, I took one step
after another,
gaining strength for the living of
an altered tomorrow.

Never will I forget how you
held me up;
never will I forget how you
stood by me.

Because of you, I can smile and
I can sing;
because of you, I can hope and
I can dream.

For all time will I
be thankful;
and every day I will pray blessings
upon you.

Dedicated to my prayer group

A STRAND OF THREE

From afar
came two friends, so dear,
to immerse themselves
in my trauma
and help me break the surface
of my grief.

Showing me
how to take small steps;
to manage errands
and solve problems
that try to wreck the routines
of life.

Their presence
brought calm, hope and peace
to erase despair
from my heartache
and ease the deep, dark troubles
of my mind.

Without them,
I could not get up
to endure sorrow
or face anger
when came the pain and weeping
of my soul.

Their friendship
game me strength to stand;
their kindness restored
my bruised spirit.
Together we became a
strand of three.

Dedicated to Pam and Terri
Ecclesiastes 4:12b

BRIDGES

What is a bridge
but a bond
between two
entities.

When the schism
that separates is
too staggering to cross,
an alliance is
needed.

And when pain and heartache
exile one from
the homeland,
a way is needed to return again
to the harbor of hope and
healing –

A way
designed by God
to escort limping hearts
across a gulf too great.

Bridges to bring
hurting souls back from
the brink of
despair.

Secure pathways
for the grief-stricken
as they walk through
the valley of
shadows.

Closing the gap
between lonely desperation
and sturdy shoulders to weep
upon.

A transfer
from the shiver of fear
to the muscle of
courage.

Crossings over the rivers
of raging emotions
to the champions of comfort and
grace.

A passage toward refuge
for the cautious and
confused.

Compassionate hands and
ever-ready feet
extending over the sea of challenges
for the weakened and the
weary.

Beautiful bridges
engineered
by God
to help hearts full of mourning
navigate the journey of
loss.

*Dedicated to friends, strangers, family
and my church.*

TEN THOUSAND MILES

WHERE YOU GO

To go
where you go
and stay where you stay,
to accept your people
as my people
and your God
as my God,
to never let
anything
separate us
but
that one thing.

And it was so.

Then Death honored
the vow
by carving a chasm
between us.

Now,
I am here
and you are
in the eternity
I one day will be.

Until then,
I wait as the
loneliness settles
about me like a
shawl
and try to live
despite
what I have
lost.

I KNOW WHAT IT'S LIKE

To wake up in the
morning and remember
that he is not here anymore.

To realize that
no matter how much I wish
or pray
I cannot bring him back.

I know what it's like to ache for
a dream in which I spend
one more day with him.

To discover that
I love him more than I thought
I did when he was alive.

I know what it's like to miss him, knowing
that I will never see him again in this life,
yet still not able to stop missing him.

To wait and
look forward to the time we
are reunited one heavenly day.

I know what it's like to move on
with my mind because I should,
but still look back with my heart
because I must.

Oh, how I know what it's like,
and because I know
I let go
of what can never be.

And I hold on to the beauty
of what once was
and take it with me,
for it is not ashes
I carry, but
a flame
fueled by a hope for tomorrow
until
finally, tomorrow becomes
the ever after
we had always longed for.

TRACES

I feel the warmth of the sun
and I remember
how he once basked in its golden glow.

I thrill to the fury of a storm
and I recall
that he, too, relished such tempests.

I wonder at the stars and their designs
and I relive
the time he taught me their names.

I listen to a song on the radio
and I smile
at how off key he sang such a song.

I laugh at the antics of a wit
and I reminisce
over the funny jokes he played on us all.

I swoon over a love story
and I weep
over losing the romance of my life.

I enjoy playing games with family and friends
and I call to mind
how he too delighted in such pastimes.

I travel the world and marvel at God's creation
and I mourn
because I miss my partner in pilgrimage.

I lend a helping hand or a shoulder to cry on
always remembering
how he gave of himself for the good of others.

I praise the Lord above and pray for those on earth
never forgetting
how he always stood beside me to worship and to pray.

I try to be patient, merciful and kind
and I think back to
how he modeled Christ-likeness every day.

I look all around me and see traces of his life
and I remember
how he lived and loved so greatly.

ONCE

Flowers on my doorstep,
Poetry on the window sill,
Sweet whispers in the morning,
A kiss he didn't have to steal.

Arms enfolding me so closely,
Laughter at our awkward dancing,
Silly singing, joking, teasing –
All a part of our romancing.

Oh, what a time of fun and dreaming,
What a life full to the brim,
What a kaleidoscope of color,
What a joy to be with him.

Then, Desolation's shroud descended
As Life's iridescence ebbed away.
Music lost all strength to comfort;
And I could not find the words to pray.

The days turned frayed and quiet
And the nights grew long and still.
Spaces yawned out loud and empty;
The air took on a lingering chill.

Time kept passing despite my sorrow –
The clock tick-tocked straight through my heart.
The world took no notice of a soul so shattered;
And the seams of my life split apart.

One day there will come a glimpsing moment
When I can look back in time and smile,
For we had love and life together
If only for just a little while.

As the years drift subtly by me
And the days turn glibly into months,
I will always stop and remember
That I was special to someone once.

OVER IT

One day, they say,
you'll get over it
and the pain will fade away.

Not so, I say,
for the hurdle is too lofty
and I haven't the power
to jump that high.

This is not a contest
or a race to the finish.

This is a new reality –
a dimension beyond the usual
heart thumpings
of life.

Spilt milk
and other such routine
memorabilia of daily
upsets
are the jots and doodles
of scratch-paper
sketches.

Sure . . . that you can
get over –
just a little hop will
do it.

But, a deluge –
and I'm not talking milk here,
you can't just mop
that up and move on.

 Ten Thousand Miles

Staring down into a
casket-filled grave
where rests the recipient of
your heart's greatest grandeur –
now that is no mere
scribble.

It is the eloquence
of an epic –
a maddening magnificence
that haunts you for time,
sans terminus.

From that day forward,
you are not who you used to be.

For each step taken,
you are one step closer to
the surreal realization
that you don't
search just the surface
for answers
anymore.

Your pursuit
has now led you toward
subterranean splendors
where faith
in the unseen
surpasses
what is seen.

Your soul's quest
has been ignited by
a heart well-acquainted
with a sorrow that
no words dare
describe.

To "get over it"
would be to turn your back
on a mirror
that is on the verge of
revealing
who you really are.

There is another way –

To let Peace
partner with you
on this journey of
heart maneuverings.

Like a tree
that offers its
spacious shade ever
the more despite carved
missives, broken branches
and embedded intrusions,
you now live
with an odyssey
etched into
your heart.

And this Odyssey
can reach out and touch
a hurting world,
helping
others to accept
instead of avoid;
to transcend
instead of descend;
to get through
instead of
get over.

Letting the Maker
mold the misery into
masterpiece.

To live
for a purpose instead of
a pastime.

Though your heart
may be brimming
with both
heaven's joy
and
a world's lament,
you now know what you
never knew before;
and you no longer need to
get over it.

Romans 8:28

INTO THE HEART

Sorrow comes into the heart,
not as an enemy,
but as a comrade who would walk
beside you,
with an arm around your
sagging shoulders
to act as a buffer
against
the sharpest stabs
of pain.

For grief must have its way
so that healing can
one day grace
the soul.

After the soil
of the heart has been
toiled and turned
by the spade of mourning,
its core is finally exposed
to the bittersweet
balm of life
continuing.

Never to forget why you grieved
or the one loved and lost,
but to remember
how to breathe deeply
and look forward
to a future that
is waiting
for you.

Knowing that
your survival honors those
who have gone
before.

One day you will notice
that sorrow
has slipped away,
only to visit from time to time
when a memory
wells up
to engulf
you.

Tears may fall to cleanse away
those few remnants of
sadness that
do linger for
awhile.

But keep walking,
for in so doing
you learn
to salute the days
ahead.

And though your heart
may not feel
like it belongs to you,
it is still yours –
just remodeled.

Let it drum onward,
for there will one day be
a renewed vision
to journey toward
and you need your heart
to meet the
challenge.

THE GIVEAWAY

Folded neatly
in storage boxes
rest his clothes.

So long have they been kept,
hidden away,
sealed in a secret shrine.

But, there is no one here
to wear them
anymore.

And so they must go.

I will take them
to a special place
where they will find
usefulness
once again; though
they shall drape
the frames of
strangers.

For, these remnants
of the past shall no longer
swathe my pain.

No more will they attire
the man I miss,
who stood tall like a hero
in a story,
the pages of which
have stopped
turning.

New tales shall be told
proclaiming
the heroics of other men
who will stand tall
for the loved ones
in their
lives.

For my consolation
I've set aside a few treasured
mementos.

Just some wardrobe misfits,
like a paint-splattered t-shirt
and a pair of worn, torn jeans.

Others brought a sparkle
to my eye, like his
flannel "lumberjack shirt"
and favorite baseball cap.

And how could I dare part with
his lilac shirt and tie
that so perfectly
complemented my
Easter dress?

After all, it took quite a bit of coaxing
to get him to wear
such a color.

Finally, I complete the sorting . . .
and the sobbing.

We take a road trip,
this special cargo and I,
in search of
new warriors to wrap.

"Good-bye" weaves its whispering
way through my mind; my heart
takes notice.

"Farewell, dear Fabric
that touched his skin,
that arrayed him so well
throughout the thread
of his life."

We arrive at last, I fear.
As I place his clothes in the care
of the wardrobe whisperers,
my heart begins its flip-flop dance
in protest.

But, I've always known this day would come –
this bittersweet finale to
a long farewell duly noted by
The Giveaway.

AFTER

The grass grows
thick and green
over the site.

The granite marker
stands not alone,
as long ago.

The scattered trees
have reached higher,
their shade broader.

Each season brings
pretty bouquets to
prove remembrance.

Through it all
love keeps kissing
each new day

Set in motion
many years before
death broke in.

For beyond us
storms brewed quietly
undetected.

But, planning for the future,
Mark always prayed
and provided.

Thinking of us,
encircling our future
with his heart.

Then the music
of his pulse
stopped playing.

But, Love refused
death's stinging deed
and burst free.

And though the warmth
of his touch has
left us,

The evidence
of his love
lives ever after.

VALENTINE

Ten years
and counting since
our wordless goodbye.

Not by our choice,
but by His –
the mystery of His will
allowing
a sudden silence.

Not understanding,
but accepting;
not despairing,
yet sorrow-ridden,
I encounter,
year after year,
a day
set aside to celebrate
adoration.

"What's a day,
anyway?" I ask myself as I gaze
upon rows of glittering endearments
and passion splattered cards.
I then bump into a battalion of
bouquets assigned the
daunting task of
depicting true
love.

My eyes glaze over.

Not to be
forgotten are
those hearts of
chocolate.
So cruel.

Ah well . . .
I find myself
surrendering to
their allure anyway.

Though the expanse
between us
cannot be measured by
human calculations,
my love for you,
Valentine
can.

It is measured
by the memories I have
of you,
enough to last
all my days.

When I think of you,
my heart
leaps,
sending a tear down
my face
and a smile to
awaken my lips.

My love
is measured by
the stories
I share about you
to all who will
listen.

 Ten Thousand Miles

Flowers
at your grave site
give testimony
to how unforgotten
you are.

Each day
I look in the mirror
and pray
that the way
I have persevered
without you would
make you proud.

Our God
knows it is only
through Him
that I continue
on without you,
while you live
in Heaven with
Him.

In my heart
my love keeps
strumming
a tune for you.

As I watch
our children live
their lives,
I see glimpses of
you in them.

And it brings you
closer.

This day of sentiments
shall pass
and come again
on every fourteenth day
of the second month,
but it is no more
noteworthy
than any other day
of the year.

For you and I are
valentined together
and nothing shall
interfere.

DAYS

If I had my way
there would have been
more of them,
lots more.

But, I have learned that
what I want and
what God wants
don't align.

I see only a grain
of sand; He sees
the whole beach
and beyond.

I count the minutes while
He measures the infinite.
Time contains me,
not Him.

We greet, grab and go,
but He does not.
Always He is
with us.

Death parts us from each
other; but in Him
it's just a
new hello.

He has His reasons and
I have mine, but
His ways are
vastly higher.

I do not understand the
allotment of our days.
He has pondered
them all.

The question "why" that badgers
is not fully answered.
It shakes faith.
Brings doubt.

The time spent with the
ones we love is
never enough.
Not ever!

But, in His Word the
numbers add up: every
hair on every
head, counted!

Before we each came to
be, our span of
life He knew –
He prepared.

For every person created, He
has a purpose – a
cherished design
for the good.

When death's day comes, we
fear. But God sees
the continuance of
His plans.

The mystery of His orchestration
transcends our every endeavor.
Through it all
He loves.

The pain of parting cuts
deep into the heart.
God dives into
this deep.

No tears fall without notice.
He catches every one
and bottles them
in mercy.

It may not make sense;
we may feel lost,
but His Grace
still stands.

Though we are acutely confounded,
He remains in control.
Not one thing
escapes Him.

At the end of life
when our time has
come, we will
see clearly.

Until that moment we must
go on. We learn
to trust and
to hope.

On our road of sorrow
He walks with us,
lifting us when
we stumble.

One day we notice our
hearts starting to mend.
We smile just
a little.

The memories don't jab us
so sharply. We look
forward, once again,
to tomorrow.

We decide to live life
in honor of those
we miss and
mourn.

At long last we welcome
the sun's warmth again.
Strength returns and
revives us.

Suddenly, the veil of fog
through which we viewed
the world vanishes
like vapor.

It hits us that the
earth's whirl never ceased.
We must jump
back on.

Days spin into months and
then years, leaving behind
the footprints of
our lives.

Ten Thousand Miles

In time we shall see
that God had been
painting beauty into
each step.

His artistry captured the essence
of every moment, no
matter the brevity
or breadth.

In the Grand Finale when
eternity triumphantly shines forth,
Truth will display
His masterpiece.

RELINQUISHMENT

Leaving –
an enigma of puzzled
emotions
the bitter entwined with the
sweet
pain embroidered with
joy
grief etched with
blessing

Unfolding
a fragile parchment
upon which stories are written
in laughter and in tears
giving breath and being
to a portrait of
hope and despair
love and . . .
a striving to refuse
hate a foothold

Then leaving
the good and the
bad
in their rightful
places
as the heart tiptoes
forward
on a path framed
with peace

Not forever
will the remnants of
tragedy
litter the walkway of this
journey

A weary soul
can shake off the
dust
from such travels
if resentment is
denied
the freedom to tag
along

Leaving
the shadows where dead dreams
are buried
where hurt burrows like a mole
in the mind
where anger tattoos the skin
of the soul
where despair slices the heart
asunder

To accept
the mercy of letting go
so we can be free
to follow
the footprints of
forgiveness

Then leaving
turns into beginning

A doorway
through which we see
the true treasures
of time spent
together

Encouraging us
to live
each new now
with
grateful wonder

Still
we must continue
leaving
yesterday after yesterday
until
tomorrow

2 Corinthians 4:18

TO FILL WITH JOY

This journey
continues until we step over
the threshold into
eternity.

All the while,
blessings bring tidings
of what we can now only
glimpse.

Sun and shadow,
cold and warmth,
hand in hand
these entities go
because each is nothing
without the other.

Meaning comes through
these opposing forces –
light verses dark,
good versus evil,
love verses hate.

To have just one
color in the spectrum
is to have no color at all.

And so I have learned
that tragedy and mercy are
yoked together and cannot
be torn asunder.

In this world
they infiltrate every
corner and cranny
of our lives,
and we live with
the aftermath, be it
jubilation or
dejection.

However, this is not
our conclusion.

For we are like prisms
whose scintillations
dazzle the mind long after
the lights go dark.

Leaving legacies
of myriad reflections
to inspire others
for good or
for evil.

And the palette
of color used
to depict
how we lived
through tragedies
and through blessings
will blend together
to paint a picture
for all to see.

Pictures
that repulse
or attract.
We each will leave
an image
in our wake.

One day
it will be evident
which artist we each chose
to give the canvas
of our life to.

For me, God has been
molding and melding,
purifying and painting for my good,
even when it appears
to be more for my
destruction.

Yes, He
has accompanied me
on this journey,
supporting me
during heartache
and leading me
toward healing
so that He can
give me life
filled with joy
instead of
despair.

Joy!
Not because
pain or sorrow
have been deleted
from my life,
but because
a loving Presence
shelters and saves me
in the midst of all
I encounter
along the way.

NO LAST WORDS

Stretching out luxuriously,
Forever beckoned.
But, Time reneged on us
without warning.

For, we had always counted on that
new tomorrow
as we took for granted living in
the present.

The minutes of our days obligingly
ticked onward,
and the hands of the clock
seemed sturdy.

Those special moments grew into
cherished memories.
Photo albums steadily stacked up into
leaning towers.

Tears and laughter intertwined
our hearts.
Nothing, we thought, could unmingle
our love.

Hand in hand we walked a
hope-filled journey with
so much treasure in our souls yet
to unlock.

But Time's agenda crashed suddenly
into ours,
toppling the pedestal upon which our
hourglass proudly stood.

The Sands scattered, inaugurating a
crystallized stillness.
Happily Ever After faltered, then just
faded away.

Togetherness was dissevered and diminished
into solitude,
leaving behind a vacuum too great
to fathom.

Robbed of those last words
never spoken,
I sank, bereft, into the agony of
mislaid moments.

A blunder took his
breath away.
No whisper, no cry, no sound
could escape.
He was gone before he knew
to speak.

So I searched ceaselessly
for clues,
like a beggar scrambling
for scraps.

Closure is illusive when there are
no goodbyes.
To be deprived of heart-mail is
heckling torture.

So, I closed my eyes and
gazed backwards.
Digging through memories brought
painful joy.

For what I uncovered
proved fateful.
Epigrams of him were everywhere
I looked.

Photos, letters, notes and home movies
spoke volumes –
testimonials telling tales of
sterling stature.

He left behind a trail of
treasured memories.
The measure of this man
rang true.

Expressions from his heart
live on
in every gift he ever gave
and in every caring gesture
he bestowed.

Past actions that prove
loving validation, and timeless
prayers to envelope us
for always.

I finally realized that
good-bye whispers, though dear,
could never have captured a lifetime of
endearing conversations.

For, embracing us all lives his
love, indisputable,
though, upon his departure, he bestowed
no last words.

DANCING GOOD-BYE

I could never dance well
in real life.

But, to my mind's eye I can
tango with abandon.

And in my imaginary world my secret weapon
is the foxtrot.

I'm so elegant in my beautiful ball gown
when I curtsy.

To disco in the highest of heels is a
piece of cake!

And I never run out of breath or drip with sweat
while riverdancing.

Of course, I need a partner for all these
complicated dance maneuvers.

A dashing prince to escort me
to the ball.

And though you are no longer here,
my dear husband,

It is for you I wait to lead me out upon
the dance floor.

For in my visions, we are never clumsy when
we twirl together.

No matter how intricate the step or quick the pace, we
stay in sync.

As we dance our romance beneath the moonglow,
we are captivating.

But alas, these are just the fantasies of a wallflower who's
lost her partner.

One day, though, we will not just be waltzing
in my dreams.

Until then, I'll just say we've simply been
dancing good-bye.

BLISTERS ON MY FEET
To Mark

In this world are wondrous
places to explore,

And many fun adventures
I choose not to ignore.

I'll need a sturdy pair of shoes
for hiking on this quest.

I'll need a map and a compass
and good places to rest.

A hat would be helpful with a
jacket or a sweater.

Waders might be necessary when
the weather gets wetter.

I'll probably need a backpack
to carry all my gear.

And a camera and a notebook
to help remember this frontier.

But, there's one detail more that
I need to make this journey.

It's not a tent, it's not a car,
it's not a lot of money.

There's no sense making such a trek
to ramble all alone.

I don't want amazing vistas
to become only my own.

 Ten Thousand Miles

A partner to tread the paths with
is what I hope to find.

With whom to share the joys, the fears,
the absences of mind.

For, life presents us all with
tempting trails to follow.

Sometimes they point to happiness,
while some make us feel hollow.

But no matter where the path goes,
no matter where it leads;

No matter if it's covered with
rocks and thorns and weeds;

No matter if we're hungry and
our clothes have turned to rags;

No matter if the path is straight
or if it just zigzags;

If I could have you by my side
at every paradox we meet,

Oh, I would walk ten thousand miles
with blisters on my feet.

EPILOGUE

TO LEAVE MY MARK

Over and over
I came face to face
with what I could not
control,
keep or
correct.

The options
were limited, the outcome
the same:
Mark would not be
coming back.

Two choices
invited my consideration:

Remain
wed to despair,
denial and bitterness,
thereby cementing
my own demise, or

Leave
everything in God's Hands
in order to secure
a better sequel.

So, I chose leaving,
but I did so with
hesitation in my heart,
tears disfiguring my face,
and the shrapnel of grief
piercing my soul.

On the pavement
of this journey,
I left the crumbs of what
I could no longer have,
and stumbled forward
into an emptiness
I did not want.

In the beginning,
I had to leave Mark
in the care of the ER
doctors and nurses.

Then I had to leave him
in intensive care
hooked up to machines
to keep him alive.

Throughout it all
I left him in God's care,
knowing the care of the doctors
would not be enough.

I had to leave him
at heaven's door
when his last breath
was imminent,
followed by
the grave
where I left him
when his earthly life
was over.

I had to leave Mark
in my memories
when I could no longer be
in his presence.

I had to leave him
in the past
when I could not bring him
into my future.

To our Father,
I had to entrust Mark
when I finally accepted
the permanence of
his absence.

I surrendered
the known for the
unknown,
feeling as if I had left myself
behind when
the concept of widowhood
overtook my
identity.

Without the presence
of Christ in my life,
I would have merely
limped along,
leaving little impact
for good
and plenty of detrimental
debris in my wake.

His arms
of healing and hope
wrapped themselves around
my heart,
slowly encouraging
a revival.

I learned to lean on Him
while He walked with me
through the tragedies and triumphs
that litter or beautify
this long and winding trail
we call life.

And so, I have been able
to leave my Mark
because God's blessings
have never failed to accompany me
on this journey,

And because I know
there shall come a day when
leaving leads to
that long-awaited Arrival,
and then
I will never have to
leave my Mark
again.

John 11:25-26
Philippians 3:20-21

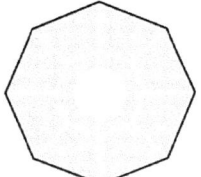

Acknowledgements

The writing of this book took seventeen years and included many pauses and times of reflection. All along the way I was accompanied by friends and family who gifted me with their love, support, comfort and prayers. Not least of these is God, who kept me always in the palm of His Hand (whether I realized it or not).

My heart is filled with gratitude for all those who helped me turn my scatterings of poetry into a book. Though I cannot specifically name you here, I thank each of you with all the gratefulness I can muster and for which I cannot find adequate expression.

My son and two daughters, my pastor and two of my dear friends provided valuable feedback throughout the process from the first draft to the final presentation. Another talented friend worked diligently to format my book and design the artwork. What a blessing you each have been to me.

List of Poems

Pathways	v
PREFACE	vii
TABLE OF CONTENTS	ix
PROLOGUE	xi
Dying Day	xi
A BEACON SHINING	1
Mark	3
Flaws, Foibles and Forbearance	8
The Twentieth Year	9
SHADOW SO DARK	11
Dilemma	13
Betrayal	16
Helpless	18
Corridors	20
Classical	22
The Final Answer	24
The Lack Of You	26
Tell Them	27
Bring Him Back	28
The Circle	30
Paper Cranes	32
Last Breath	33
The Unclasping	35
The Plead	36
Walking Out	38
Untitled	40
Altar	41
Until	42
Every Shovelful of Dirt	43
Boxed In	45
Gossamer Shadow	47
Blank	48
Alone	49
The Coffee Cup	50
Bringing Flowers	53
The Land of My Grief	55

DELUGE & DESERT THUNDER & ICE — 57

Deserted Island	59
Residue	60
Never Again	61
Not Ever!	64
The Downward Groove	65
Waves	67
No Longer	68
Woe	72
Out of Order	73
Pretty Things	74
A Closet Full of Rags	76
The Cold Place	79
Tears in a Bottle	84
Pulling Strings	86
Let the Pain Begin!	87
Noble Song	88
Hurting	90
Feel	92
Anger	96
Blame	98
Appraisal, Part One	99
The Precipice	100
Call It Like It Is	102
Relics of Grief	104
In the Heavens of My Heart	105

AN ACCOUNTING — 107

Weeds	109
The Chamber	113
Accountable	115
Deposition	118
Arbitration	120
Value	122
Revenge	124

REFUGE & RESCUE — 127

Prayer — 129
God in the Hurt — 131
Punishment Syndrome, Part One — 135
Punishment Syndrome, Part Two — 137
Running — 138
Break Through — 139
Like a Thief — 140
Keeping My Heart — 142
Released — 143
Time — 145
The Loudest Thing — 146
Cling — 148
For Us — 150
Fistful — 153

HOPE RECLAIMED — 155

Solitaire, I Thought — 157
Hope — 159
Regrets — 161
Grieve — 164
Appraisal, Part Two — 166
Letting Go — 167
Not Anymore — 171
Comfort — 172
Turn Around — 174
The Dark Grey — 176
Moving On — 178
No Broken Tomorrow — 179

GRATITUDE — 183

The Work of Their Hands — 185
The Nurses — 186
Because of You — 187
A Strand of Three — 189
Bridges — 190

TEN THOUSAND MILES — 193

- Where You Go — 195
- I Know What It's Like — 196
- Traces — 198
- Once — 200
- Over It — 202
- Into the Heart — 206
- The Giveaway — 208
- After — 211
- Valentine — 213
- Days — 217
- Relinquishment — 222
- To Fill with Joy — 225
- No Last Words — 229
- Dancing Good-Bye — 232
- Blisters on My Feet — 234

EPILOGUE — 237

- To Leave My Mark — 239

Acknowledgements — 245
LIST OF POEMS — 247
About The Author — 255

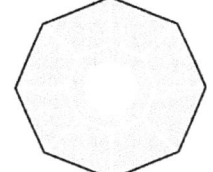

About the Author

Eloria Elliot was born and raised in the Midwest. She graduated from university with a B.A. in English. Eloria met Mark while working on her degree, and they married soon after graduation. She worked as a technical writer for three years, after which she became a full-time mother, eventually of three children.

Eloria and Mark moved periodically, following Mark's work assignments. They lived in the southern United States, England, and finally settled on the west coast of the US. Tragedy struck shortly after this last move, and thus began the long journey that culminates in this book.

When she's not writing or reading, Eloria enjoys traveling, being in nature, and spending time with her family and friends. She continues to live on the west coast, near two of her children, one of her four grandchildren, and her many friends who have loved and supported her throughout the years.

eloria@eloria-elliot.com

www.ingramcontent.com/pod-product-compliance
Lightning Source LLC
Chambersburg PA
CBHW070839160426
43192CB00012B/2241